VGM Careers for You Series

CAREERS FOR

GENIUSES
& Other
Gifted Types

Jan Goldberg

W9-DAJ-899

VGM Career Books
NTC/Contemporary Publishing Group

Library of Congress Cataloging-in-Publication Data

Goldberg, Jan.
    Careers for geniuses & other gifted types / Jan Goldberg.
        p. cm. — (VGM careers for you series)
      ISBN 0-658-00464-6 (cloth). — ISBN 0-658-00465-4 (pbk.)
      1. Science—Vocational guidance.   2. Technology—Vocational
guidance. 3. Arts—Vocational guidance. I. Title: Careers for
geniuses and other gifted types. II. Title. III. Series.
  Q147.G63   2000
  502.3—dc21   00–38158
                                                CIP

Published by VGM Career Books
A division of NTC/Contemporary Publishing Group, Inc.
4255 West Touhy Avenue, Lincolnwood (Chicago), Illinois 60712-1975 U.S.A.
Copyright © 2001 by NTC/Contemporary Publishing Group, Inc.
Printed in the United States of America
International Standard Book Number: 0-658-00464-6 (hardcover)
                                     0-658-00465-4 (paperback)

01 02 03 04 05 06 LB 19 18 17 16 15 14 13 12 11 10 9 8 7 6 5 4 3 2 1

*This book is dedicated to
the memory of my
beloved parents,
Sam and Sylvia Lefkovitz.
Your inspiration lives on.*

Contents

Acknowledgments

The author gratefully acknowledges:

- The numerous professionals who graciously agreed to be profiled in this book

- My dear husband, Larry, for his inspiration and vision

- My children—Sherri, Deborah, and Bruce—for their encouragement and love

- Family and close friends—Adrienne, Marty, Mindi, Cary, Michele, Paul, Michele, Alison, Steve, Marci, Steve, Brian, Steven, Jesse, Colin, Andrew, Bertha, and Aunt Helen—for their kindness and support

- Diana Catlin for her insights and input

- Betsy Lancefield and Denise Betts, editors at VGM, for making all projects rewarding and enjoyable

Genius Defined by the Gifted

The simplest schoolboy is now familiar with truths for which Archimedes would have sacrificed his life. ERNEST RENAN

*P*ainters, sculptors, musicians, scientists, engineers, computer scientists, mathematicians, doctors, and astronauts. What do they all have in common? For many of us, the words *genius* or *gifted* would come to mind. Though there might not be total agreement on the definition of the word *genius*, most dictionaries define a genius as someone who has exceptionally great natural ability. Does this sound like you?

While it is true that these special individuals may be found following a wide variety of career paths, some fields particularly lend themselves to geniuses. The fields I have chosen to include in this book are biological sciences, medicine, agricultural sciences, physical sciences, invention, aeronautics, engineering, computer science, mathematics, music, and art.

Here are some perspectives on genius from a number of people who might themselves be rightfully considered to be a part of this category.

Geniuses are like thunderstorms. They go against the wind, terrify people, cleanse the air. SØREN KIERKEGAARD

Genius is not so much about new ideas as it is about clarity of ideas. Two people can have the same idea yet it will be genius in the one and mediocrity in the other. KEVIN SOLWAY

Genius is the ability to act rightly without precedent—the power to do the right thing the first time. ELBERT HUBBARD

The ability of someone to choose and arrange the details of their creative field guided by a vision is a major hallmark of a genius. JOHN BRIGGS

Neither a lofty degree of intelligence nor imagination nor both together go to the making of genius. Love, love, love, that is the soul of genius. WOLFGANG A. MOZART

The first and last thing required of genius is the love of truth. JOHANN WOLFGANG VON GOETHE

A man of genius makes no mistakes. His errors are the portals of discovery. JAMES JOYCE

Genius . . . is the capacity to see ten things where the ordinary man sees one. EZRA POUND

Genius not only diagnoses the situation but supplies the answers. ROBERT GRAVES

The principal mark of a genius is not perfection but originality, the opening of new frontiers. ARTHUR KOESTLER

It is impossible that a genius—at least a literary genius—can ever be discovered by his intimates; they are so close to him that he is out of focus to them and they can't get at his proportions; they can't perceive that there is any considerable difference between his bulk and their own. MARK TWAIN

The world is always ready to receive talent with open arms. Very often it does not know what to do with genius. OLIVER WENDELL HOLMES

Genius is the ability to reduce the complicated to the simple. C. W. CERAN

Genius is that energy which collects, combines, amplifies, and animates. SAMUEL JOHNSON

These are the prerogatives of genius: to know without having learned; to draw just conclusions from unknown premises; to discern the soul of things. AMBROSE BIERCE

Genius is one percent inspiration and ninety-nine percent perspiration. ATTRIBUTED TO THOMAS EDISON

Great geniuses have the shortest biographies. Their cousins can tell you nothing about them. They lived in their writings, and so their house and street life was trivial and commonplace. RALPH WALDO EMERSON

A fine genius in his own country is like gold in the mine. BENJAMIN FRANKLIN

Geniuses are commonly believed to excel other men in their power of sustained attention. . . . But it is their genius making them attentive, not their attention making geniuses of them. WILLIAM JAMES

Genius is no snob. It does not run after titles or seek by preference the high circles of society. WOODROW WILSON

Genius is not a single power. . . . It reasons, but it is not reasoning; it judges, but it is not judgment; it imagines, but it is not imagination; it feels deeply and fiercely, but it is not passion. It is neither, because it is all. EDWIN PERCY WHIPPLE

CHAPTER ONE

Careers in the Biological Sciences

The whole of science is nothing more than a refinement of everyday thinking. ALBERT EINSTEIN

Help Wanted—Research Scientist

Are you looking for a job . . . or for an opportunity?

Our corporation seeks talented and driven individuals to join its research team developing the next generation of genetic analysis tools. Based in Connecticut and founded on technology licensed from a nearby university, we seek individuals who share our vision of building a world-class organization that will significantly impact humanity through biotechnology. We offer competitive compensation along with excellent benefits, including a 401(k) plan, health insurance, and health club membership in addition to the opportunity for equity participation.

We seek a research scientist who will drive the development of our core technologies through the design, execution, and analysis of experiments and assist in the development of intellectual property for the company. Publication of research findings in peer-reviewed journals will be strongly encouraged.

You must possess expert knowledge of molecular biology and cloning technology with a broad understanding of genetics, biochemistry, and instrumentation. Qualified candidates will possess excellent communication, laboratory, and computational skills. A proven research and publication record and strong analytical skills are necessary. Requires Ph.D. in molecular biology, cell biology, genetics, or related field. Postdoctoral and/or industry experience an advantage but not required. For immediate consideration, please send your resume by mail, fax, or E-mail.

Welcome to the World of Biological Scientists

Biological scientists are devoted to studying living organisms and their relationships to their environments. Many biological scientists work in the area of research and development. Some conduct basic research to increase our knowledge of living organisms. Others, in applied research, use knowledge provided by basic research to develop new medicines, increase crop yields, and improve the environment.

Biological scientists who conduct research usually work in laboratories using electron microscopes, computers, thermal cyclers, and a wide variety of other equipment. Some of these professionals may conduct experiments on laboratory animals or greenhouse plants.

A number of biological scientists perform a substantial amount of research outside of the laboratory. For example, botanists may conduct research in tropical rain forests to determine what plants grow there, or ecologists may study how forest areas recover after a fire.

Most biological scientists who come under the broad category of biologist can be further classified by the types of organisms they study or by the specific activities they perform, although some of the recent advances in the understanding of basic life processes at the molecular and cellular levels have blurred some traditional classifications.

Aquatic Biologists

Aquatic biologists study plants and animals that live in water. *Marine biologists* study saltwater organisms, and *limnologists* study freshwater organisms. Marine biologists are sometimes erroneously called oceanographers, but oceanography usually refers to the study of the physical characteristics of oceans and the ocean floor.

Biochemists

Biochemists study the chemical composition of living things. They try to understand the complex chemical combinations and reactions involved in metabolism, reproduction, growth, and heredity. Much of the work in biotechnology is done by biochemists and molecular biologists because this technology involves understanding the complex chemistry of life.

Botanists

Botanists study plants and their environments. Some study all aspects of plant life; others specialize in areas such as identification and classification of plants, the structure and function of plant parts, the biochemistry of plant processes, the causes and cures of plant diseases, and the geological ancestry of plants.

Microbiologists

Microbiologists investigate the growth and characteristics of microscopic organisms such as bacteria, algae, or fungi. Medical microbiologists study the relationship between organisms and disease or the effect of antibiotics on microorganisms. Other microbiologists may specialize in environmental, food, agricultural, or industrial microbiology, virology (the study of viruses), or immunology (the study of mechanisms that fight infections). Many microbiologists use biotechnology as they advance knowledge of cell reproduction and human disease.

Physiologists

Physiologists study life functions of plants and animals, both in the whole organism and at the cellular or molecular level and under normal and abnormal conditions. Physiologists may specialize in functions, such as growth, reproduction, photosynthesis, respiration, or movement, or in the physiology of a certain area or system of the organism.

Zoologists

Zoologists study animals—their origins, behaviors, diseases, and life processes. Some experiment with live animals in controlled or natural surroundings, while others dissect dead animals to study their structures. Zoologists are usually identified by the animal group they study; for instance, ornithologists focus on birds, mammalogists on mammals, herpetologists on reptiles, and ichthyologists on fish.

Ecologists

Ecologists study the relationship among organisms and between organisms and their environments and the effects of influences such as population size, pollutants, rainfall, temperature, and altitude.

Medical Scientists

Biological scientists who do biomedical research are usually called medical scientists. Medical scientists working on basic research delve into the functioning of normal biological systems in order to understand the causes of and to discover treatment for diseases and other health problems. Medical scientists often try to identify the kinds of changes in a cell, chromosome, or gene that signal the development of medical problems, such as different types of cancer. After identifying structures of or changes in organisms that provide clues to health problems, medical scientists may then work on the treatment of problems.

For example, a medical scientist involved in cancer research might try to formulate a combination of drugs that will lessen the effects of the disease. Medical scientists who have a medical degree might administer the drugs to patients in clinical trials, monitor their reactions, and observe the results. (Medical scientists who do not have medical degrees normally collaborate with medical doctors who deal directly with patients.) The medical scientists might then return to the laboratory to examine the results and, if necessary, adjust the dosage levels to reduce negative side effects or to try to induce even better results. In addition to using basic research to develop treatments for health problems, medical scientists attempt to discover ways to prevent health problems from developing, such as affirming the link between smoking and increased risk of lung cancer or alcoholism and liver disease.

Moving Forward

Advances in basic biological knowledge, especially at the genetic and molecular levels, continue to spur the field of biotechnology forward. Using this technology, biological and medical scientists manipulate the genetic material of animals or plants, attempting to make organisms more productive or disease resistant. The first application of this technology occurred in the medical and pharmaceutical areas. Many substances not previously available in large quantities are now beginning to be produced by biotechnological means, and some may be useful in treating cancer and other diseases. Advances in biotechnology have opened up research opportunities in almost all areas of biology, including commercial applications in agriculture and the food and chemical industries.

Education and Training

Biological scientists who intend to teach at the college leve,l perform independent research, or serve as administrators are generally required to earn doctoral degrees. Usually master's degrees are sufficient for some jobs in applied research and for jobs in management, inspection, sales, and service. Bachelor's degrees will suffice for some nonresearch jobs.

Sometimes, graduates with bachelor's degrees are able to work in laboratory environments on their own projects, or they may find work as research assistants. Others become biological technicians, medical laboratory technologists, or (with courses in education) high school biology teachers. Many with bachelor's degrees in biology enter medical, dental, veterinary, or other health profession schools.

Most colleges and universities offer bachelor's degrees in biological science and many offer advanced degrees. Curricula for advanced degrees often emphasize a subfield such as microbiology or botany, but not all universities offer all curricula. Advanced degree programs include classroom and fieldwork, laboratory research, and a thesis or dissertation. Biological scientists who have advanced degrees often take temporary postdoctoral research positions that provide specialized research experience. In private industry, some biological scientists may become managers or administrators; others leave biology for nontechnical managerial, administrative, or sales jobs.

A doctorate in a biological science is the minimum education required for prospective medical scientists because the work of medical scientists is almost entirely research oriented. This degree qualifies one to do research on basic life processes or on particular medical problems or diseases and to analyze and interpret the results of experiments on patients. Medical scientists who administer drug or gene therapy to human patients, or who otherwise interact medically with patients (such as drawing blood, excising tissue, or performing other invasive procedures), must have a medical degree. It is particularly helpful for medical scientists to earn both doctoral and medical degrees.

In addition to a formal education, medical scientists are usually expected to spend several years in postdoctoral positions before they are offered permanent jobs. Postdoctoral work provides valuable laboratory experience, including a background in specific processes and techniques (such as gene splicing) that is transferable to other research projects later on. In some institutions, the postdoctoral position can lead to a permanent position.

Employment Outlook

Despite prospects of faster-than-average job growth from now through 2006, biological and medical scientists can expect to face considerable competition for coveted basic research positions. More biological scientists will be needed to determine the environmental impact of industry and government actions and to prevent or correct environmental problems. Expected expansion in research related to health issues—such as AIDS, cancer, Diabetes, and Alzheimer's disease—should also result in growth.

However, much research and development, including many areas of medical research, is funded by the federal government. Anticipated budget tightening could lead to smaller increases in research and development expenditures, further limiting the dollar amount of each grant and slowing the growth of the number of grants awarded to researchers. If, at the same time, the number of newly trained scientists continues to increase at the present rate, both new and established scientists will experience greater difficulty winning and renewing research grants.

Earnings

The Bureau of Labor Statistics reports that the median annual earnings for biological scientists is about $50,000. Median salaries for all other life scientists is about $47,000. For medical scientists, median annual earnings are about $57,000. Scientists employed by the federal government generally earn even higher salaries.

Parade of Professionals

Amadeo J. Pesce, Ph.D., Professor of Pathology

Dr. Pesce serves as the director of the toxicology laboratory and professor of experimental medicine at the University of Cincinnati Hospital. He has been associated with the University of Cincinnati for more than twenty years.

"I always knew I was interested in medical research," Dr. Pesce says. "So that's where I was focused early on. I earned my undergraduate degree at the Massachusetts Institute of Technology. Then I attended Brandeis University for my graduate degree in biochemistry. My postdoctoral scholarship was at the University of Illinois at Champaign-Urbana.

"To do this kind of work, you need to have Ph.D. credentials. I also have board certification from the American Board for Clinical Chemistry, which I think is very important. (Certification is given to those who have the proper scientific background, five years of experience in the field, and successful completion of an examination.)

"In most cases I work as part of a team of researchers," says Dr. Pesce. "The composition of the team may change depending on the project. Participants may include postdoctoral fellows, part-time or full-time technologists, pathologists, mathematicians, psychiatrists, substance-abuse counselors, and other health and scientific professionals.

"Usually there are several projects going on at the same time. For instance, we're now helping with the clinical trials in developing methods of measurement for a couple of different projects. One project is to help pace patients by monitoring the effectiveness of the drug called AZT, which is used in the treatment of AIDS. We've developed the technology to measure the concentration of drugs inside the cell and are working very closely with the clinician and the clinical trials that are being conducted.

"Another project we're participating in is the study of developing agents that will help combat substance abuse by reducing the craving and the other aspects that make people want to continue to use drugs. In this project, we work with a group of psychiatrists and substance-abuse counselors, and they provide specimens from the patients for us to monitor.

"In addition to the hours spent in the laboratory, a considerable portion of my time is spent thinking and writing. One must think things through and be able to communicate them effectively and efficiently in order for the research to have meaning. As I *always* tell my students, if it's not written down, it was never done.

"As an administrator, I have other responsibilities: I supervise a postdoctoral fellow and handle personnel issues and administrative problems. And at this point in my life, I accomplish this and keep fairly regular working hours. But when I was younger (and for many years), I worked from seven in the morning until ten at night, five days a week. The other two days, I *only* worked eight to ten hours a day. This was not required but just my own enthusiasm showing, based upon my decision to be one of the four most-recognized authorities in the field. So I set on a path of learning all I could and then proceeded to put out a series of books (eighteen) about the field. This required an immense amount of work. I tell everyone that I did this to become rich and famous (my children always told me to skip the fame). But as it turns out, all I got was the fame. However, even though I didn't make the money I had hoped for, it has still been very rewarding. Fans as far away as Australia have asked me to sign their copies of my books.

"This career has many other rewards. Uppermost is the accomplishment of developing a theory and finding supporting data. (After all, projects are funded grants for which you must show results by a certain date in order to be funded for the next project). On the downside, the worst part of the job is when you write a paper and it gets rejected by your peers (and you think they're wrong, and in fact you know they're wrong). However, the real issue for me is that we've done some pioneering work for people that has proved to be quite fruitful and rewarding.

"Here's an example. A while back we developed a way of looking at cancer in mice, and a colleague working on cancer research sent me a letter commending me on the work. The fact that somebody would think enough of our work to take what we've done and build on it is very flattering.

"Another accomplishment relates to transplant patients. Some of the drugs used to treat these patients are very expensive, and we were able to devise a way of cutting the cost of those drugs from about $6,000 a year to about $1,200. This means that Third World countries can actually afford the drug for their transplant patients. That's quite an improvement!

"To be successful in this career, it helps to have an understanding partner, as I did. And since it is so important to be able to interact with people, exchange ideas, and get them to help with particular areas of your project, you must have the ability to get along with all kinds of people. You have to be aware of what issues others have and be able to accommodate them so they'll accommodate you in return. I have found that this is the proper approach to a successful collaboration. It's not unlike working with others on a book or any other project in which a number of people need to extend themselves in order to fulfill a common goal."

H. Graham Purchase, Ph.D., Veterinary Medical Researcher

Dr. Purchase is the director of veterinary medical research at Mississippi State University.

"I was born in Rhodesia (now Zimbabwe), educated in Kenya, East Africa, and received my university training in South Africa. My father, also a veterinarian who worked in research, always said that since animals feed on plants, it's wise to learn about the plant world before going to veterinary school. So I went to college when I was sixteen and earned a bachelor's degree in botany. Following this, I completed my veterinary degree in South Africa, practiced for two years, and then fulfilled my dream of coming to the United States to do research. While employed here, I earned a master's and a doctorate at Michigan State University (majoring in microbiology and public health). It took eight years to complete my doctorate, but it was well worth it.

"I started my research in a poultry laboratory in East Lansing, Michigan, and after a few years, met an American girl, married her, and decided to become a citizen of the United States. I worked at the poultry research laboratory, performing research on tumor viruses of poultry species, for about thirteen years. And this was one occasion where I can absolutely say that I was definitely at the right place at the right time because the laboratory discovered the cause of one of the most economically devastating poultry diseases of the world (Market's disease, a form of cancer) and created a vaccine that would prevent the disease. The first commercially applicable cancer vaccine ever developed, it was initially patented and used in the United States extensively. Now it's used worldwide. This period was the most exciting and rewarding of my life.

"As a 'bench' researcher, I examined the cultures of cells in which we grew the disease-causing viruses or the vaccine that prevented the disease. Routinely I would go to the necropsy room and find those birds that had died in the experiments. I would open those birds and examine what they died from to verify that it was not something else unrelated to the experiment. The rest of the day would involve writing up manuscripts and grant proposals. Often, I took work home with me because I couldn't get it done during the daytime hours.

"After thirteen years, I moved into administration and was offered a job in Washington, D.C. I spent fourteen years there in nine different jobs in research administration. The research was in a variety of areas: plant, animal, human nutrition, family economics, soil, and water. But I have a great interest in veterinary research, and when the opportunity presented itself here at Mississippi State in the College of Veterinary Medicine, I took it. Here we do research on the prime commodities of Mississippi, which include one of our big income producers—catfish—and our number-one product—poultry.

"As a research administrator, a typical day here involves interacting with many individuals one-on-one," says Dr. Purchase. "I handle the budget of the college, so often there are budget forms and various commitment forms to sign—for example, allowing individuals to travel, enabling people to buy new equipment, permitting staff to be hired. There are also manuscripts and proposals to review to make sure they're suitable. We are accredited by the American Association for the Accreditation of Laboratory Animal Care, which has very high standards of review for all experiments on animals. Every single experiment that involves animals has to be reviewed by an animal care and use committee to make sure that the animals are not harmed unnecessarily. Also the accreditation involves making sure that the facilities are maintained, so that is another area of concern for me.

"A good part of my day is devoted to meetings with my superiors to inform them about how the research projects are progressing. Frequently I have visitors to escort through our research facilities. I have reports to prepare on the research that we are doing, most of which are lay reports for general use for administrators and the legislators. The actual writing of the research itself is done by the faculty. Our system is set up so that a designated faculty member will write the proposals, then the manuscripts will be sent out for peer review to make sure that the conclusions are supported by the data, and so on. I orchestrate that review process.

"We have many levels of researchers working here. Generally speaking, the principal investigators, or leaders (those who actually design the experiments), have doctoral credentials. But we also have a number of technicians, some with master's degrees, others with bachelor's degrees. We also have animal caretakers and animal technicians—some of them have technician degrees while others are only high school graduates. In addition, we have quite a number of students working toward bachelor's degrees who do laboratory cleanup here in order to gain some experience in the field. Then we have graduate students and individuals who already have their bachelor's degrees who are going on to get their master's or doctoral degrees. These students spend a good deal of the time with their major professors learning how to conduct experiments and do research, so that when they graduate they'll know how to perform these tasks independently.

"If your grades are good, if you perform well during examinations, and if you can become an expert in your area, research is a wonderful career. It's challenging and very innovative. I enjoy the ability to develop something and to find out new things. But it's very rigorous, too.

"Most of my researchers are not here from nine to five. They arrive here early in the morning, they frequently miss their lunch breaks, and they take work home at night or come in at night and on weekends to keep their work going. Research means pushing forward the frontiers of science, and to succeed, you must be trained, prepared, and dedicated to putting in the necessary hours and effort."

For More Information

For information on careers in biochemistry, contact:

American Society for Biochemistry and Molecular Biology
9650 Rockville Pike
Bethesda, MD 20814

For information on careers in the biological sciences, contact:

American Institute of Biological Sciences
1444 I Street NW, Suite 200
Washington, DC 20005
http://www.aibs.org

For information on careers in biotechnology, contact:

Biotechnology Industry Organization
1625 K Street NW, Suite 1100
Washington, DC 20006

For information on careers in botany, contact:

Botanical Society of America
Business Office
1735 Neil Avenue
Columbus, OH 43210
http://www.botany.org

For information on careers in microbiology, contact:

American Society for Microbiology
Office of Education and Training—Career Information
1325 Massachusetts Avenue NW
Washington, DC 20005
http://www.asmusa.org

For information on careers in physiology, contact:

American Physiological Society Education Office
9650 Rockville Pike
Bethesda, MD 20814
http://www.faseb.org/aps

Information on acquiring a job as a biological scientist with the federal government may be obtained from the Office of Personnel Management through a telephone-based system. Consult your telephone directory under U.S. Government for a local number. Information is also available from the Internet site at http://www.usajobs.opm.gov.

Information on federal job opportunities is available from local offices of state employment services or offices of the U.S. Office of Personnel Management, located in major metropolitan areas.

CHAPTER TWO

Careers in Medicine

Medicine, the only profession that labors incessantly to destroy the reason for its own existence. JAMES BRYCE

> *Help Wanted—Physician*
> Our group is seeking a gifted, knowledgeable, compassionate, and experienced pediatrician to add additional support, strength, and depth to our wonderful team of doctors. Please respond immediately.

Perhaps in no other profession do we wish to have geniuses congregate more than in the field of medicine. No other field has a greater effect on our daily lives than that of medicine. Don't you want to believe that your doctors are all geniuses?

Welcome to the World of Medicine

There are two basic types of physicians—the M.D., doctor of medicine, and the D.O., doctor of osteopathic medicine. M.D.s are also known as allopathic physicians. While M.D.s and D.O.s may use all accepted methods of treatment, D.O.s put special emphasis on holistic care, preventative medicine, and the body's musculoskeletal system.

Primary care physicians, including those who focus on general and family medicine, general internal medicine, or general pediatrics, account for about one-third of all M.D.s. When we get sick (or simply want to stay well), we consult these professionals first. Thus, primary care physicians tend to see the same patients over and over.

General and family practitioners emphasize comprehensive health care for patients of all ages and for the family as a whole. General internists provide care mainly for adults who have a wide range of problems associated with the body's organs. General pediatricians focus on children's health.

When necessary, primary care physicians refer patients to specialists, who are experts in a variety of medical areas, such as neurology, obstetrics and gynecology, orthopedics, or cardiology. D.O.s are more likely to be primary care providers than allopathic physicians, although they can be found in all specialties.

Specialists

The American Medical Association reports the following breakdown of specialties among physicians:

aerospace medicine—.1 percent

allergies—.5 percent

anesthesiology—4.6 percent

cardiovascular diseases—2.6 percent

child psychiatry—.8 percent

colon and rectal surgery—.1 percent

dermatology—1.2 percent

diagnostic radiology—2.7 percent

emergency medicine—2.7 percent

forensic pathology—.1 percent

gastroenterology—1.3 percent

general and family medicine—10 percent

general internal medicine—16 percent

general pediatrics—7 percent

general preventive medicine—.2 percent

general surgery—5.2 percent

neurological surgery—.7 percent

neurology—1.6 percent

nuclear medicine—.2 percent

obstetrics and gynecology—5.2 percent

occupational medicine—.4 percent

ophthalmology—2.4 percent

orthopedic surgery—3.1 percent

otalaryngology—1.3 percent

pathology—2.5 percent

pediatric cardiology—.2 percent

physical medicine and rehabilitation—.8 percent

plastic surgery—.8 percent

psychiatry—5.3 percent

public health—.2 percent

pulmonary diseases—1 percent

radiology—1.1 percent

radiation oncology—.5 percent

thoracic surgery—.3 percent

urological surgery—1.4 percent

other specialties—1 percent

unspecified/unknown/inactive—14.4 percent.

On the Job

The working life of a doctor is a difficult one. Doctors are usually required to work long days with irregular hours. They must often travel from their private offices to the hospitals with which they are affiliated in order to treat their patients. In addition, they may be called upon for emergency situations at any time of day or night. Even when they are not seeing patients, they may spend a good part of their time advising patients who call with various medical concerns and complaints. And, of course, they are required to make life-and-death decisions at a moment's notice.

About 70 percent of all doctors work out of an office (including HMOs and clinics). About another 20 percent are employed by hospitals, and the remaining percentages practice in the federal government—most in Department of Veterans Affairs hospitals and clinics or in the Public Health Service of the Department of Health and Human Services.

The northeastern and western states have the highest ratio of physicians to population; the south central states have the lowest ratio. D.O.s are more likely than M.D.s to practice in small cities and towns and in rural areas. M.D.s tend to locate in urban areas, close to hospital and educational centers.

Osteopathic physicians locate chiefly in states that have osteopathic schools and hospitals. In a recent survey, about one-half of them were found to be practicing in six states: New Jersey, Ohio, Pennsylvania, Michigan, Florida, and Texas.

Education and Training

Prospective doctors must be cognizant of the reality that becoming a doctor requires many, many years of formal study. This usually translates to four years of undergraduate school, four years of medical school, and three to eight years of internship and residency, depending on the specialty selected. In some instances, medical schools offer a combined undergraduate and medical school program that lasts six years instead of the usual eight years.

Premedical students must complete undergraduate work in physics, biology, mathematics, English, organic and inorganic chemistry, social sciences, and humanities. Additionally, they often volunteer at local medical facilities in order to get a step ahead and gain some valuable practical experience.

The minimum educational requirement for entry to a medical or osteopathic school is three years of college. However, most applicants have at least a bachelor's degree. In fact, many have advanced degrees. Getting accepted to a medical school is no easy task. There are many qualified candidates, so competition is keen.

In most cases, institutions instruct applicants to submit transcripts, scores from the Medical College Admission Test (MCAT), and letters of recommendation. They also take into account elements such as leadership qualities, strength of character, personality, and participation in extracurricular and volunteer activities. Most schools require an interview with a member of the admissions committee.

Most of the first two years of medical school is spent in laboratories and classrooms, taking courses in anatomy, biochemistry, physiology, pharmacology, psychology, microbiology, pathology, medical ethics, and laws governing medicine. The prospective physicians also learn to take medical histories, examine patients, and diagnose illnesses.

During their last two years, students work with patients under the supervision of experienced physicians in hospitals and clinics. Through rotations in internal medicine, family practice, obstetrics and gynecology, pediatrics, psychiatry, and surgery, they gain valuable experience in the diagnosis and treatment of illness.

Following medical school, almost all M.D.s enter a residency —graduate medical education—in a specialty that takes the form of paid on-the-job training. This is usually in a hospital. After graduating, most D.O.s serve a twelve-month rotating internship. Then they enter residencies that may last two to six years. Residences in managed care settings may be a distinct advantage since they provide experience with this increasingly common type of medical practice.

Before being allowed to practice medicine, doctors in all states, plus the District of Columbia and U.S. territories, must meet mandatory licensing requirements. To be licensed, physicians must graduate from an accredited medical school, pass a licensing examination, and complete one to seven years of graduate medical education. Although physicians licensed in one state can usually get a license to practice in another without further examination, some states limit reciprocity. Graduates of foreign medical schools can qualify for a license after passing an examination and completing a residency in a U.S. hospital.

Physicians who wish to specialize are required to engage in additional training. Depending on the specialty, M.D.s and D.O.s may spend up to an additional seven years seeking board certification in a specialty. A final examination immediately after residency, or after one or two years of practice, is also necessary for board certification by the American Board of Medical Specialists (ABMS) or the American Osteopathic Association (AOA). There are twenty-four specialty boards, ranging from allergy and immunology to urology. For certification in a subspecialty, physicians usually need another one to two years of residency.

On a personal level, individuals who wish to become physicians must have a desire to serve patients, be self-motivated, and be able to survive the pressures and long hours of medical education and practice. Physicians must also have a good bedside manner, emotional stability, and the ability to make difficult decisions in emergencies.

Becoming a doctor is financially draining. And while the cost of education has increased, student financial assistance has not. As a result, more than 80 percent of medical students borrow money to cover their expenses.

Employment Outlook

Due to continued expansion within the health care industry, employment of physicians is expected to accelerate at a faster pace than average. The growing and aging population will prompt overall growth, and new technologies will permit more intensive care. As a result, physicians can do more tests, perform more procedures, and treat conditions previously regarded as untreatable. Job prospects will be particularly good for primary care physicians—general and family practitioners, general pediatricians, and general internists—and for specialists in geriatrics and preventive care.

However, because of efforts to control health care costs and increased reliance on utilization guidelines that often limit the use of specialty services, a lower percentage of specialists will be in demand. At the same time, the number of specialists continues to grow. Competition for specialists' jobs will be especially keen in large urban and suburban areas and for those who work directly for hospitals, such as anesthesiologists and radiologists.

Earnings

Earnings for physicians are among the highest for any occupation. According to the American Medical Association, median income, after expenses, for allopathic physicians is about $160,000. The middle 50 percent earn between $115,000 and $238,000. Self-employed physicians—those who own or are part owners of their medical practices—have higher median incomes than salaried physicians. Earnings vary according to number of years in practice; geographic region; hours worked; and skill, personality, and professional reputation.

According to the Association of American Medical Colleges, the average salaries of medical residents range from approximately $33,000 (for those in their first year of residency) to about $42,000 (for those in their sixth year).

Parade of Professionals

Lawrence C. Newman, M.D.

Dr. Lawrence Newman is the director of the Headache Institute at St. Luke's–Roosevelt Hospital Center in New York. He received his B.A. from Clark University in Worcester, Massachusetts, his M.A. in biology in 1979, and his M.D. from the Universidad Autonoma de Guadalajara, Mexico, in 1983. He did his residency in internal medicine in Elmhurst Hospital Center in Queens, New York; a residency in neurology at Albert Einstein College of Medicine in the Bronx, New York; served as chief resident in neurology at Albert Einstein College; and received a Headache Fellowship at Montefiore Medical Center in the Bronx.

"I knew that I would be a doctor from the age of five or six," he says. "I thought that my pediatrician was a wonderful person.

I used to make gifts for him in school and actually looked forward to office visits. In fact, while I was in college, I spent my summers doing research in his lab.

"My great uncle Nat was also an inspiration to me. He was, and probably still is, the best physician I have ever met. He was a fantastic diagnostician, had a wonderful bedside manner, and was a true gentleman. Upon his retirement, his patients all got together and organized a surprise party for him to show their appreciation. One of my biggest thrills was having my uncle attend one of my lectures and remark that he actually learned something!

"My original belief was that I was going to be a pediatrician. And throughout medical school, I still maintained that belief. During my training, however, I learned a lot about myself. While I enjoyed treating children and interacting with them while they were healthy, I had a very hard time treating children who were very ill. Many nights I would come home and cry. I realized I could not do this for the rest of my life.

"I also discovered that the field of neurology was fascinating. The different parts of the nervous system—the brain, spinal cord, and peripheral nerves—make up a complicated network. Determining where the problem lay was like figuring out a puzzle—I could tell exactly what part was injured by closely examining the patient. But headaches hold a special attraction for me. Patients with headaches are usually young and otherwise totally healthy. Nonetheless, their lives have been totally disrupted by these painful attacks, as have the lives of those around them—their families, friends, neighbors, and coworkers. Added to this, most patients with headaches are not properly treated by their physicians and are often misunderstood and left to suffer needlessly. Trying to figure out what type of headache the patient has is a challenge that I really enjoy. Since there are about three hundred medical conditions that have headache as a symptom, it can be challenging. Also trying to determine the correct treatment—not everything works for everybody with the same condition—is also an intriguing aspect of my profession. But the greatest part is helping people to stop their suffering and get back to their lives.

"My job has many different parts; some are more enjoyable than others. The best parts of my job involve taking care of patients. I see patients in my office four days a week from ten in the morning until five in the afternoon. I take a history first and ask them a lot of questions about their headaches and their health. Then I examine them and set up a treatment plan to help them get rid of the attacks and also to treat attacks when they occur. I also have rooms in my office to treat patients who develop pain at home and don't get relief from the medications they are taking. I can treat them with injectable medications or even set up an intravenous treatment.

"I am also involved in clinical trials in which I test promising new medications before they are approved for use. These studies help to prove if these medications work well and show if they are safe or not. Another part of my job that I really like is education. Not only do I get to teach my patients, but I frequently lecture to medical students, doctors in training, and practicing doctors about the newest and best ways to treat patients with headaches. I also get to write book chapters and journal articles about the work I have been doing and to present the findings of my work at large medical conferences throughout the world.

"Sometimes the work is stressful—especially on the days when the patients aren't doing well. There are a lot of telephone calls to answer, even after the office closes, because people can get sick anytime—daytime, nighttime, even holidays.

"Though I don't enjoy the very long hours that often don't leave me enough time to spend with my family, there is no job I would rather do. I have never had any regrets. The hours are long, the work is stressful, and the training needed to be a doctor takes so many years (four years of college, four years of medical school, and then five years of training), but I would do it all again. Being a physician is everything I imagined it would be when I as a kid looking up to my pediatrician and my uncle.

"My advice to others would be not to give up. Always try new avenues. Because so many people were trying to get into medical school when I applied, it was very difficult. So I went out of the country. Many of my friends gave up and went into business. That would definitely have been a mistake for me. So just keep going!"

Robert S. Gotlin, M.D.

Dr. Robert Gotlin is director of orthopedic and sports rehabilitation, Department of Orthopedic Surgery at Beth Israel Medical Center in New York. He earned a B.S. from the State University of New York at Stony Brook in Long Island, then attended the National College of Chiropractic Medicine in Lombard, Illinois, and Southeastern University of the Health Sciences in Miami, Florida. He is also an assistant professor of rehabilitation at the Albert Einstein College of Medicine of Yeshiva University in New York.

"A passion for helping others and having a respected career are the general undertones that helped me choose a career in medicine," says Dr. Gotlin. "Orthopedic and sports is the specific track I chose due to my passion for exercise and fitness. As a physician, mastering interpersonal skills is a fundamental characteristic that cannot be overstated as a foundation for success. Many people possess many different personalities, so it has always been my belief that no two people are alike, and each person must be treated as an individual.

"Keeping busy and being creative fuel my day as a practicing physician. The gratifying look on my patients' faces when they are relieved of pain or free from weakness is what keeps me going. The ability to be creative and dynamic is inherent to medicine as it is described as both an art and a science. Change is the nature of the beast, so one must be open-minded and always ready for new ideas and methods for treatment.

"The typical day for me is lengthy and extensive, starting at 5:30 A.M. and ending when my body poops out. Patient care, research, literature reviews, and practice management are intimately integrated with family duties, including coaching seven youth sports teams and extensive community youth sports development commitments. All in all, this brings a smile to my face.

"Dedicating one's career to helping others can be a most gratifying experience and accomplished via many avenues. For me, medicine is the vehicle to travel the avenue to help those in need. Of particular interest to me are the intriguing aspects of fitness and sports medicine. By and large, caring for a health-conscious population in orthopedic and sports rehabilitation enables me not only to treat ailments but also to educate, guide, and influence people's everyday lifestyles in a positive way.

"For whichever career one chooses, it is easier to successively accomplish goals when one has a personal passion for that particular interest. So many times during life, obstacles alter the direction one is traveling, and if the glass of water on the table is viewed as half full rather than half empty, achieving goals is more likely. I strongly urge any individual to learn about and experience firsthand the day-to-day demands for a chosen field. Then ask, 'Where and what will I be doing ten years from now?' If there is uncertainty, rethink the career choice. If there is certainty and a real passion for that career, the answer to this question will easily be answered. To this day, fifteen years into my career, my passion is as strong as ever, and the drive into work is still something I look forward to."

For More Information

For a list of allopathic medical schools and residency programs, as well as general information on premedical education, financial aid, and medicine as a career, contact:

American Medical Association
515 North State Street
Chicago, IL 60610

Association of American Medical Colleges
Section for Student Services
2450 N Street NW
Washington, DC 20037
http://www.aamc.org

For general information on osteopathic medicine as a career, contact:

American Osteopathic Association
Department of Public Relations
142 East Ontario Street
Chicago, IL 60611
http://www.am-osteo-assn.org

American Association of Colleges of Osteopathic Medicine
5550 Friendship Boulevard, Suite 310
Chevy Chase, MD 20815
http://www.aacom.org

CHAPTER THREE

Careers in the Agricultural Sciences

Scientific discovery and scientific knowledge have been achieved only by those who have gone in pursuit of it without any practical purpose whatsover in view. MAX PLANCK

Help Wanted—Food Scientist

Serve as food scientist in the Space Food Systems laboratory at one of the country's space centers, developing food products for use on board the International Space Station. Conduct research and development activities supporting the shelf-life extension of shelf-stable bakery products used in space flight. Create and maintain food-system documentation, including food manufacturing specifications.

Candidate must possess an M.S. in food science with a minimum of four years of industry experience in the area of food product development. Also must possess a basic knowledge of analytical laboratory equipment and procedures.

Salary commensurate with experience. Apply on-line.

Welcome to the World of Agricultural Science

The work of agricultural scientists plays an important part in maintaining and increasing the nation's agricultural productivity. Agricultural scientists study farm crops and animals and develop ways of improving their quantity and quality. They look

31

for techniques to conserve soil and water, ways to improve crop yield and quality with less labor, and avenues to control pests and weeds more safely and effectively. They research methods of converting raw agricultural commodities into attractive and healthy food products for consumers.

Agricultural science is closely related to biological science, and agricultural scientists use the principles of biology, chemistry, and other sciences to solve problems in agriculture. They often work with biological scientists on basic biological research projects, or they may concentrate on applying the technological advances to agriculture.

Many agricultural scientists work in basic or applied research and development. Others manage or administer research and development programs or manage marketing or production operations in companies that produce food products or agricultural chemicals, supplies, and machinery. Some agricultural scientists are consultants to business firms, private clients, or government agencies.

Depending on the agricultural scientist's area of specialization, the nature of the work performed varies.

Food Science

Food scientists or technologists are usually employed in the food processing industry, at universities, or by the federal government. They help meet consumer demand for food products that are healthful, safe, palatable, and convenient. To accomplish this, they use their knowledge of chemistry, microbiology, and other sciences to develop new or better ways of preserving, processing, packaging, storing, and delivering foods. Some engage in basic research, discovering new food sources; analyzing food content to determine levels of vitamins, fat, sugar, or protein; or searching for substitutes for harmful or undesirable additives, such as nitrites. Many food technologists work in product development. Others enforce government regulations, inspecting food processing areas and ensuring that sanitation, safety, quality, and waste management standards are met.

Plant Science

Plant science includes the disciplines of agronomy, crop science, entomology, and plant breeding, among others. These scientists study plants and their growth in soils, helping producers of food, feed, and fiber crops to continue to feed a growing population while conserving natural resources and maintaining the environment. Agronomists and crop scientists not only help increase productivity, but also study ways to improve the nutritional value of crops and the quality of seed. Some crop scientists study the breeding, physiology, and management of crops and use genetic engineering to develop crops resistant to pests and drought.

Soil Science

Soil scientists study the chemical, physical, biological, and mineralogical composition of soils as they relate to plant or crop growth. They study the responses of various soil types to fertilizers, tillage practices, and crop rotation. Many soil scientists who work for the federal government conduct soil surveys, classifying and mapping soils. They provide information and recommendations to farmers and other landowners regarding the best use of land and how to avoid or correct problems such as erosion. They may also consult with engineers and other technical personnel working on construction projects about the effects of, and solutions to, soil problems. Since soil science is closely related to environmental science, soil scientists also apply their knowledge to ensure environmental quality and effective land use.

Animal Science

Animal scientists develop better, more efficient ways of producing and processing meat, poultry, eggs, and milk. Dairy scientists, poultry scientists, animal breeders, and other related scientists study the genetics, nutrition, reproduction, growth, and development of domestic farm animals. Some animal scientists inspect and grade livestock or food products, purchase livestock, or work in technical sales or marketing. As extension agents or consultants, animal scientists advise agricultural producers on how to upgrade animal housing facilities properly, lower mortality rates, or increase production of animal products, such as milk or eggs.

An entomologist might deliver presentations to local farmers about insect problems in growing corn and other crops.

Education and Training

Training requirements for agricultural scientists depend on the specialty and the type of work they perform. A bachelor's degree in agricultural science is sufficient for some jobs in applied research or in assisting in basic research, but a master's or doctoral degree is required for basic research. A doctoral degree in agricultural science is usually needed for college teaching and for advancement to administrative research positions. Degrees in related sciences such as biology, chemistry, or physics or in related engineering specialties also may qualify persons for some agricultural science jobs.

All states have a land-grant college that offers agricultural science degrees. Many other colleges and universities also offer agricultural science degrees or some agricultural science courses. However, not every school offers all specialties. A typical undergraduate agricultural science curriculum includes communications, economics, business, and physical and life sciences courses, in addition to a wide variety of technical agricultural science courses. For prospective animal scientists, these technical agricultural science courses might include animal breeding, reproductive physiology, nutrition, and meats and muscle biology. Students preparing to become food scientists take courses such as food chemistry, food analysis, food microbiology, and food processing operations. Those preparing to be crop or soil scientists take courses in plant pathology, soil chemistry, entomology, plant physiology, and biochemistry, among others. Advanced degree programs include classroom and fieldwork, laboratory research, and a thesis based on independent research.

Agricultural scientists should be able to work independently or as part of a team and be able to communicate clearly and concisely, both orally and in writing. Most agricultural scientists also need an understanding of basic business principles.

Agricultural scientists who have advanced degrees usually begin in research or teaching. With experience, they may advance to jobs such as supervisors of research programs or managers of other agriculture-related activities.

Employment Outlook

Employment of agricultural scientists is expected to grow about as fast as the average for all occupations through the year 2006. Additionally, the need to replace agricultural scientists who retire or otherwise leave the occupation permanently will account for many more job openings than projected growth.

Generally speaking, those with advanced degrees will be in the best position to enter jobs as agricultural scientists. However, competition for teaching positions in colleges or universities and for some basic research jobs may be keen, even for doctoral holders. Federal and state budget cuts may limit funding for these positions through the year 2006.

Earnings

According to the United States Bureau of Labor Statistics, agricultural and food scientists earn about $45,000 per year.

Parade of Professionals

Carl. I. Evensen, Ph.D., Assistant Extension Specialist

Dr. Evensen serves as assistant extension specialist for natural resource management and environmental quality in the Department of Agronomy and Soil Science at the University of Hawaii in Honolulu.

"All my life, I have enjoyed gardening and growing crops, so the decision to go into agriculture as a profession seemed very natural to me. I also like working with other people and have found that I truly enjoy agricultural extension work, since it combines these interests and inclinations.

"After I earned my bachelor's degree in biology from Whitman College in Walla Walla, Washington, I was still very unsure of what I wanted to do as a profession. I decided that to give myself some time to think and to try to give back something to other people, I would join the Peace Corps. So I spent two years in Kenya working as a horticultural extensionist in an isolated part of the Coast Province called the Taita Hills. This was a wonderful, life-changing experience, which convinced me that I wanted to work in agriculture but also pointed out the gaps in my knowledge.

"I then determined that I would go back to school to study agriculture and decided on the strong tropical agriculture program at the University of Hawaii. My master's program was spent studying agroforestry in Hawaii, while my doctoral research was performed in Indonesia, working on a soil management project. These studies gave me a strong background in soil fertility and crop nutrition, which I continue to use in my current job. Also, these overseas work experiences really broadened my perspective and helped me tremendously in understanding the needs of foreign graduate students. My subsequent job as an agronomist (1989–1993) at the Hawaii Sugar Planter's Association (HSPA) was very valuable in giving me experience with large-scale plantation agriculture as a contrast to my previous work with small-scale subsistence farmers. Also at HSPA, I began to work with soil and water conservation issues and problems.

"My current job is extremely variable," says Dr. Evensen. "Most of my time is spent on extension-related activities, which involve planning trainings for extension agents (the faculty in the field who work most closely with farmers), speaking at and attending meetings with other government agencies and private industry, conducting teacher trainings, and making presentations at public events. Every day is different and holds its own challenges and rewards. I also seek grant funding and have led five projects in the last four years, mostly dealing with demonstrations of soil conservation, pesticide reduction, and education on pollution control. Of course there are also administration and reporting requirements with all of these activities.

"Some days are spent entirely in my office, either on the phone or at my computer, writing reports, summarizing data, responding to E-mail or correspondence. Other days (my favorites) are spent entirely in the field, teaching or collecting data in a field project. Usually, several days a month are spent traveling to neighboring islands to meet with agents and farmers or to participate in trainings. It also seems that I spend an inordinate amount of time (at least several hours or sometimes several days a week) in various meetings, either at the university or with various interagency groups.

"I also teach two graduate classes (Agriculture and the Environment and Sustainable Agriculture) and am developing a new undergraduate course, Environmental Issues. To prepare for this, I spend weeks selecting readings and discussion topics and planning the course syllabus. Once the course has begun, I review the materials before each session and try to keep up with current related topics to bring up in class. I also am a committee member on a number of graduate student committees. So, I also have both scheduled and unscheduled meetings with the students to discuss their projects. A great deal of time is also required for preparation and grading of comprehensive exams, reading and commenting on the student's thesis or dissertation, and then participating in the final defense.

"I really enjoy the variety of activities and many new challenges I face every day. Teaching and working with graduate students are among the most enjoyable and challenging things that I do. However, I also really enjoy getting out in the field to work on a project or to work with farmers and agents. My less enjoyable responsibilities include reporting and project administration. Also, I sometimes get overwhelmed when a number of planned activities and unplanned requests or requirements coincide.

"I feel this type of job is very rewarding but also overwhelming and all consuming. It is important to be organized and frequently reprioritize the multiple and changing activities so that the really critical things get done in a timely manner. However, it is also very important to avoid becoming consumed by the job. You must make time for yourself and your family in order to avoid becoming burned out."

Michael Moore, Ph.D., Taxonomist

Dr. Moore serves as the curator of the Plant Department at the University of Georgia.

"As an undergraduate at the University of Georgia, I was already interested in this field. So I stayed on as a graduate student and earned my master's degree in 1985 and my doctorate in

1989. I was lucky enough to get a job at the university even before I finished school. I've been the curator of the Herbarium (plant museum) in the Plant Department of the University of Georgia for three years.

"Taxonomists can do many things. But you should realize that a master's degree is usually required and a doctorate is preferred for those who wish to assume this career. If you wish to focus on academia, you can do research as well as teach. Then you would want a heavy background in molecular biology and similar course work. If you want to be more of a field botanist—that is, someone who does more or less what I do in herbaria—or work with a private company protecting endangered species, you would want to have more ornamental horticulture training.

"The Herbarium at the University of Georgia is the largest in the state of Georgia," relates Dr. Moore. "We have just over two hundred thousand mounted specimens. My responsibilities as curator are to make sure that the collection is well maintained and curated in a proper manner. Then, I also have research projects that take me out into the field. This past year, for instance, I was out in the field every other week between March and October. I enjoy the fact that I work both inside and outdoors.

"As a curator, I also have a responsibility to respond to questions from the public. Additionally, I exchange specimens with other herbaria, loan plants, and handle plant identifications as they come in. In addition, I have also taught some classes at the university from time to time.

"Most major universities do have herbaria. The number of curators they have will depend on how many specimens they house. For example, in very large herbaria there will be individual curators who will be responsible for certain species of categories of plants.

"There are a number of hot topics that require the services of professionals in this field: conservation of the rain forest and environmental issues, for example. In the future, I am quite sure that there will still be jobs for those who have a good basic background in taxonomy and are able to do basic field research."

Art Davis, Ph.D., Cereal Chemist

Dr. Davis is the director of scientific services at the American Association of Cereal Chemists, where he has served for the past two years.

"I obtained my bachelor's degree from Oregon State University and spent two years in the Peace Corps. Then I went on to graduate school at Kansas State University, where I earned a master's and a doctorate in cereal chemistry. I knew I was always headed into biology and the sciences.

"After working for Pillsbury Company in its research and development department, I assumed a position heading a research group for the American Institute of Baking for about two and a half years. Following that, I served on the faculty of Kansas State University for nine years. Subsequent positions included quality assurance manager for General Foods Bakeries and three years as the director of technical services for the Green Giant Fresh Vegetables Group.

"Here at the American Association of Cereal Chemists, the main thing we do is offer about thirty short courses and other continuing education programs," explains Dr. Davis. "Whenever there's a need to provide basic information in food science, we fill that void. For instance, there's been a tremendous growth in the use of frozen foods in this country in recent years, and a lot of (particularly smaller) companies are interested in getting into that field. Since there was no training available, we went out and found some people who were knowledgeable about this topic and put together a two-day course that provides the basics for those who need this information.

"Other courses we offer include water activity, wet milling sensory analysis, food technology, batter and breading technology, chemical leavening, breakfast cereal technology, chemistry technology, and principles of cereal science. Individuals often come to us with biology, microbiology, or engineering backgrounds but no experience with food. So for individuals both overseas and here in the States, our courses provide the information needed.

"Another service we provide is an international check sample service. At regular intervals—monthly, bimonthly, or quarterly—samples that have been submitted to us by our clients are sent to participating laboratories. Specific analysis is performed and the results are forwarded to us. We then compile all of the results and provide a report that reveals the status of perhaps a hundred laboratories. This gives the labs some idea of whether or not they are in line with other labs and how accurate their findings are. In fact, this year we're starting to do some proficiency certification. If you send all of the samples in for a year and your results are in line with the other labs, we'll issue you a certificate verifying that fact.

"Because there's a critical size that must be reached before it's feasible to establish your own research and development group, smaller companies tend to depend on their suppliers to do their research and development for them. For instance, my experience at the General Foods Bakeries taught me that you can mix doughnut batter, starting with flour, sugar, salt, and so forth, but because of some of the peculiarities of putting doughnut mixes together, it's a lot more efficient to buy a mix from a company that makes doughnut mixes. If you've got a problem with it, you can ask them to solve it, or if you want something a little bit different, you can ask them to create that for you. Flavor houses, mix suppliers, and fats and oils suppliers have their own research and development divisions, as do some of the bakers and mills. These are the people who can get you the properties you want. Thus, they'll go into their labs and massage the molecules until they come up with what you are looking for.

"For those interested in getting into food science, I would highly recommend Kansas State University's Department of Grain Science and Industry. The undergraduate program, which includes serious chemistry, physics, and a little bit of engineering course work, is so excellent that almost every student who graduates invariably receives at least a few job offers. There is also a graduate program that provides a strong background and solid job offers for its graduates.

"If you are planning on doing research at a university, I'd recommend that you get a doctorate. However, industry doesn't get terribly hung up on degrees. I know a number of good researchers with master's degrees who have gone on and done quite well. I even know of a few with bachelor's degrees who have distinguished themselves. If you are an able researcher, there are opportunities out there for you."

Brent Steven Sipes, Ph.D., Assistant Plant Pathologist

Dr. Sipes is employed by the University of Hawaii's Department of Plant Pathology in Honolulu. He came to the university as a junior researcher in 1991 to evaluate pineapple for resistance or tolerance to a plant parasite.

"I very much enjoy the outdoors and plants," says Dr. Sipes. "As a child, I was encouraged to garden by my next door neighbor, a grandmotherly teacher. This interest in plants and their biology, systematics, and cultivation has followed me ever since.

"Majoring in plant pathology, I received my B.S. degree from Purdue University in West Lafayette, Indiana, in 1983. With the same specialty, I earned my M.S. and Ph.D. from North Carolina State University in Raleigh, North Carolina, in 1987 and 1991, respectively.

"Growing up in the sixties and seventies, I was also very conscientious about environmental stewardship. This activism motivated me to help in the proper use of pesticides to avoid problems that seemed to plague agricultural production. Becoming a plant pathologist (someone who studies plant diseases and their control) was a natural outgrowth.

"My first job was in a commercial greenhouse in Louisville, Kentucky. We grew roses that were shipped all over the Midwest. We had to regularly treat the plants with chemicals to ensure acceptable quality and maintain production. This was a fun job but physically exhausting and taught me that I didn't want to be a common laborer the rest of my life.

"I spent three college summers working in a premier institute, the Morton Arboretum, located in a suburb of Chicago. I was tutored by professional horticulturists who cared about plants and their well being. These people instilled within me the desire to perform quality work that would ensure that future generations would enjoy the plants in the collections of the arboretum. I learned much about plant classification—what makes a rose a rose and a maple a maple, rather than an oak.

"I did well in college and knew before graduation that I would pursue an advanced degree. Graduate school agreed with me. I enjoyed the thrill of collecting and analyzing data from experiments and from formulating and asking questions. I enjoyed conducting research.

"Now, as an assistant professor, my days can vary greatly," Dr. Sipes says. "Some days are spent indoors moving from one committee meeting to the next. Other days I spend at my desk analyzing and preparing data for presentations. Perhaps the best days are those when I am in the field collecting samples, setting up a test, or treating an experiment. Some days I get to travel to experiments on neighboring islands. I even attend scientific meetings held all over the world.

"I have a great deal of flexibility as to the order of my day. I like to start early while the day is cool, around 7:00 A.M. and finish before it gets really hot, by 3:30 or 4:00 P.M., even if I am inside all day. Because 60 percent of my work involves field experiments, much of the work depends upon the weather. Rain can really ruin our best plans. Consequently, sometimes the work is very slow and easy, whereas other times everything needs to be done and there is hardly any time to take a breath.

"I work between forty-eight and fifty hours per week. Since I enjoy my job, I usually don't keep track of the hours. I work with many different types of people—senior professors, administrators, technical staff who assist me in my research, and students. Each group is different, and the challenge is to work well with each one. The people in my laboratory are much like a family. We get along well together, although we may not always share the same opinions.

"What I like most about my work is the ability to pose questions and contemplate how to answer them. I like the freedom to choose my own path. I like to analyze data to answer those questions. I am honored by the respect my work affords me in the community.

"If you are interested and excited by this career, then commit yourself to it. The most important aspect to living is to enjoy your livelihood. Do not work to live on the weekends."

For More Information

Information on careers in agricultural science is available from:

American Society of Agronomy
Crop Science Society of America
Soil Science Society of America
677 South Segoe Road
Madison, WI 53711

Food and Agricultural Careers for Tomorrow
Purdue University
1140 Agricultural Administration Building
West Lafayette, IN 47907

For information on careers in food technology, write to:

Institute of Food Technologists
221 North LaSalle Street, Suite 300
Chicago, IL 60601

For information on careers in entomology, contact:

Entomological Society of America
9301 Annapolis Road
Lanham, MD 20706

Information on acquiring a job as an agricultural scientist with the federal government may be obtained from the Office of Personnel Management through a telephone-based system. Consult your telephone directory under U.S. Government for a local number. Information is also available from the Internet site at http://www.usajobs.opm.gov.

CHAPTER FOUR

Careers in the Physical Sciences

I shall make electricity so cheap that only the rich can afford to burn candles. THOMAS A. EDISON

Help Wanted—Scientist

Our company is a global leader in the discovery, manufacture, and marketing of innovative specialty chemicals. Our high-quality products place the company at the cutting edge.

We are seeking qualified candidates to coordinate, direct, and perform analytical activities involving complex problems in support of research, development, regulatory affairs, and technical support. As an ideal candidate, you must have strong verbal and communications skills to interact with internal and external customers and be adept at sample handling and preparation, as well as flexible to handle assignments in various areas. Additionally, you must possess academic or industrial experience across multiple fields. Your level of education and experience will determine the position level. Salary is commensurate with experience. We offer excellent benefits and incentives.

Senior Scientist: Requires a Ph.D. in chemistry or equivalent and up to two years' relevant experience or an M.S. and five to ten years' experience. *Scientist II:* Requires an M.S. in chemistry or equivalent and three to six years' experience or a B.S. and five to ten years' experience. *Scientist I:* Requires an M.S. in chemistry or equivalent or technical discipline and one to four years' relevant experience or a B.S. in chemistry or technical discipline and three to six years' relevant experience. *Associate Scientist:* Requires an M.S. in chemistry or equivalent or technical discipline and up to two years' experience or a B.S. and seven years' experience.

Welcome to the World of Physical Science

Chemists

Without chemists, we would live in a world without paints, synthetic fibers, drugs, cosmetics, electronic components, and a thousand other products. Chemists search for and put to practical use new knowledge about chemicals. Although chemicals are often thought of as artificial or toxic substances, all physical things, whether naturally occurring or of human design, are composed of chemicals.

Many chemists work in research and development. In basic research, chemists investigate the properties, composition, and structure of matter and the laws that govern the combination of elements and reactions of substances. In applied research and development, they create new products and processes or improve existing ones, often using knowledge gained from basic research. For example, synthetic rubber and plastics resulted from research on small molecules uniting to form large ones (polymerization).

Chemists also work in production and quality control in chemical manufacturing plants. They prepare instructions that specify ingredients, mixing times, and temperatures for each stage in the process. They also monitor automated processes to ensure proper product yield, and they test samples to ensure they meet industry and government standards.

Chemists often specialize in a subfield. *Analytical chemists* determine the structure, composition, and nature of substances and develop analytical techniques. In addition, they identify the presence and concentration of chemical pollutants in air, water, and soil. *Organic chemists* study the chemistry of the vast number of carbon compounds. Many commercial products, such as drugs, plastics, and fertilizers, have been developed by organic chemists. *Inorganic chemists* study compounds consisting mainly of elements other than carbon, such as those in electronic components. *Physical chemists* study the physical characteristics of atoms and molecules and investigate how chemical reactions work. Their research may result in new and better energy sources.

Physicists and Astronomers

If you are interested in exploring the forces of nature, consider a career as a physicist. Using observation and analysis, physicists explore and identify basic principles governing the structure and behavior of matter, the generation and transfer of energy, and the interaction of matter and energy. Some physicists use these principles in theoretical areas, such as the nature of time and the origin of the universe; others apply their physics knowledge to practical areas such as the development of advanced materials, electronic and optical devices, and medical equipment.

Physicists design and perform experiments with lasers, cyclotrons, telescopes, mass spectrometers, and other equipment. They also find ways to apply physical laws and theories to problems in nuclear energy, electronics, optics, materials, communications, aerospace technology, navigation equipment, and medical instrumentation.

Most physicists work in research and development. Some do basic research to increase scientific knowledge. Physicists who conduct applied research build upon the discoveries made through basic research and work to develop new devices, products, and processes. For instance, basic research in solid-state physics led to the development of transistors and then to the integrated circuits used in computers.

Physicists also design research equipment. This equipment often has additional unanticipated uses. For example, lasers are used in surgery; microwave devices are used for ovens; and measuring instruments can analyze blood or the chemical content of foods.

Physicists generally specialize in one of many subfields—elementary particle physics, nuclear physics, atomic and molecular physics, physics of condensed matter (solid-state physics), optics, acoustics, plasma physics, or the physics of fluids. Some even specialize in a subdivision of one of these subfields; for example, within condensed matter physics, specialties include superconductivity, crystallography, and semiconductors.

Since all physics involves the same fundamental principles, specialties may overlap, and physicists may switch from one subfield to another. Also, growing numbers of physicists work in combined fields, such as biophysics, chemical physics, and geophysics.

Astronomy is sometimes considered a subfield of physics. Astronomers use the principles of physics and mathematics to learn about the fundamental nature of the universe, including the sun, moon, planets, stars, and galaxies. They also apply their knowledge to problems in navigation and space flight.

Primarily involved in research, astronomers analyze large quantities of data gathered by observatories and satellites and then write scientific papers or reports on their findings. Most astronomers spend only a few weeks each year making observations with optical telescopes, radio telescopes, and other instruments.

Geologists and Geophysicists

Have you always been fascinated by rocks and stones? Do you find it impossible to walk by an interesting specimen without picking it up? Perhaps you are a good candidate to become a geologist or geophysicist!

Geology and geophysics are closely related fields, but there are major differences. Geologists study the composition, structure, and history of the earth's crust. They try to find out how rocks were formed and what has happened to them since their formation. Geophysicists use the principles of physics and mathematics to study not only the earth's surface, but also its internal composition, ground and surface waters, atmosphere, and oceans as well as its magnetic, electrical, and gravitational forces. Both geologists and geophysicists, however, commonly apply their skills to the search for natural resources and to the solution of environmental problems.

Geologists and geophysicists examine chemical and physical properties of specimens in laboratories. They study fossil remains of animal and plant life or experiment with the flow of water and oil through rocks. Some geological scientists play an important role in preserving and cleaning up the environment through designing and monitoring waste disposal sites, preserving water supplies, and locating safe sites for hazardous waste facilities and landfills.

Geoscientists working in the oil and gas industry sometimes process and interpret the maps produced by remote sensing satellites to help identify potential new oil or gas deposits. Seismic technology is also an important exploration tool. Seismic waves are used to develop three-dimensional computer models of underground or underwater rock formations.

Geologists and geophysicists also apply geological knowledge to engineering problems in constructing large buildings, dams, tunnels, and highways. Some administer and manage research and exploration programs; others become general managers in petroleum and mining companies.

There are numerous subdisciplines or specialties that fall under the two major disciplines of geology and geophysics that further differentiate the kind of work geoscientists do. For example, *petroleum geologists* explore for oil and gas deposits by studying and mapping the subsurface of the ocean or land. *Mineralogists* analyze and classify minerals and precious stones according to composition and structure. *Paleontologists* study fossils found in geological formations to trace the evolution of plant and animal life and the geologic history of the earth. *Stratigraphers* help to locate minerals by studying the distribution and arrangement of sedimentary rock layers and by examining the fossil and mineral content of such layers. Individuals who study marine geology are usually called *oceanographers* or *marine geologists*. They study and map the ocean floor and collect information using remote sensing devices aboard surface ships or underwater research craft.

Geophysicists may specialize in areas such as geodesy, seismology, or marine geophysics, also known as physical oceanography. *Geodesists* study the size and shape of the earth, its gravitational field, tides, polar motion, and rotation. *Seismologists* interpret data from seismographs and other geophysical instruments to detect earthquakes and locate earthquake-related faults. *Physical oceanographers* study the physical aspects of oceans, such as currents and the interaction of sea surface and atmosphere.

Hydrology is a discipline closely related to geology and geophysics. *Hydrologists* study the distribution, circulation, and physical properties of underground and surface waters. They study the form and intensity of precipitation, its rate of infiltration into the soil, its movement through the earth, and its return to the ocean and atmosphere. The work they do is particularly important in environmental preservation and remediation.

Meteorologists

If you have always been obsessed with the weather and what is going on in the heavens above, then meteorology is for you!

Meteorologists study the atmosphere's physical characteristics, motions, processes, and the way it affects the rest of our environment. The best-known application of this knowledge is in forecasting the weather. However, weather information and meteorological research also are applied in air-pollution control, agriculture, air and sea transportation, defense, and the study of trends in the earth's climate (such as global warming or ozone depletion).

Meteorologists who forecast the weather, known professionally as *operational meteorologists*, are the largest group of specialists. They study information on air pressure, temperature, humidity, and wind velocity, and they apply physical and mathematical relationships to make short- and long-range weather forecasts. Their data comes from weather satellites, weather radar, and remote sensors and observers in many parts of the world. These forecasts inform not only the general public but also industries such as shipping, aviation, agriculture, fishing, and utilities that need accurate weather information for both economic and safety reasons.

The use of weather balloons, launched several times a day, to measure wind, temperature, and humidity in the upper atmosphere, is supplemented by far more sophisticated weather equipment that transmits data as frequently as every few minutes. Doppler radar, for example, can detect rotational patterns in violent storm systems, allowing forecasters to better predict the occurrence, direction, and intensity of thunderstorms, tornadoes, and flash floods.

Some meteorologists work in research. *Physical meteorologists*, for example, study the atmosphere's chemical and physical properties; the transmission of light, sound, and radio waves; and the transfer of energy in the atmosphere. They also study factors affecting the formation of clouds, rain, snow, and other weather phenomena, such as severe storms. *Climatologists* collect, analyze, and interpret past records of wind, rainfall, sunshine, and temperature in specific areas or regions. Other research meteorologists examine the most effective ways to control or diminish air pollution or improve weather forecasting using mathematical models.

Weather stations are found all over the country—in airports, in or near cities, and in isolated and remote areas. Some meteorologists also spend time observing weather conditions and collecting data from aircraft.

Education and Training

Chemists

A bachelor's degree in chemistry or a related discipline is usually the minimum education necessary to work as a chemist. However, a high percentage of research jobs require a doctoral degree.

Many colleges and universities offer bachelor's degree programs in chemistry, many of which are approved by the American Chemical Society (ACS). Several hundred colleges and universities also offer advanced degree programs in chemistry.

Students planning careers as chemists should enjoy studying science and mathematics and should like working with their hands building scientific apparatuses and performing experiments. In addition to required courses in analytical, inorganic, organic, and physical chemistry, undergraduate chemistry majors usually study biological sciences, mathematics, and physics. Computer courses are invaluable, as employers increasingly prefer job applicants to be not only computer literate but able to apply computer skills to modeling and simulation tasks. Laboratory instruments are also computerized, and the ability to operate and understand equipment is essential.

Because research and development chemists are increasingly expected to work on interdisciplinary teams, some understanding of other disciplines, including business and marketing or economics, is desirable, along with leadership ability and good oral and written communication skills. Experience, either in academic laboratories or through internships or co-op programs in industry, also is useful. Some employers of research chemists, particularly in the pharmaceutical industry, prefer to hire individuals with several years of postdoctoral experience.

In government or industry, beginning chemists with bachelor's degrees work in technical sales or services, quality control, or assist senior chemists in research and development laboratories. Some may work in research positions, analyzing and testing products, but these may be technicians' positions, with limited upward mobility. Many employers prefer chemists with doctorates to work in basic and applied research. A doctorate is also generally preferred for advancement to many administrative positions.

Many people with bachelor's degrees in chemistry enter other occupations in which a chemistry background is helpful, such as technical writing or chemical marketing. Some enter medical, dental, veterinary, or other health profession schools.

Chemistry graduates may become high school teachers, and those with doctorates may teach at the college or university level. However, they usually are then regarded as science teachers, or college or university faculty, rather than as chemists. Others may qualify as chemical engineers, especially if they have taken some courses in engineering.

Physicists and Astronomers

A doctoral degree is the common educational requirement for physicists and astronomers because most jobs are in research and development. Additional experience and training in a post-doctoral research assignment, although not required, is helpful in preparing for permanent research positions.

The same level of education would also be required (in most cases) for the many physicists and astronomers who ultimately take jobs teaching at the college or university level. Those who hold bachelor's or master's degrees in physics are rarely qualified to fill positions as physicists. They are, however, usually qualified to work in an engineering-related area or other scientific fields, to work as technicians, or to assist in setting up laboratories. Some may qualify for applied research jobs in private industry or nonresearch positions in the federal government. Often, master's degrees are sufficient to land teaching jobs at two-year colleges.

Hundreds of colleges and universities offer bachelor's degrees in physics. Undergraduate programs provide a broad background in the natural sciences and mathematics. Typical physics courses include mechanics, electromagnetism, optics, thermodynamics, atomic physics, and quantum mechanics.

About two hundred colleges and universities have physics departments that offer doctorates in physics. Graduate students usually concentrate in a subfield of physics, such as elementary particles or condensed matter. Many people begin studying for their doctorates immediately after their bachelor's degrees.

About forty universities offer the doctoral degree in astronomy, either through an astronomy department, a physics department, or a combined physics/astronomy department. Applicants to astronomy doctoral programs face keen competition for available slots. Those planning a career in astronomy should have a very strong physics background. In fact, an undergraduate degree in physics is excellent preparation, followed by a doctorate in astronomy.

Mathematical ability, computer skills, an inquisitive mind, imagination, and the ability to work independently are important traits for anyone planning a career in physics or astronomy. Prospective physicists who hope to work in industrial laboratories applying physics knowledge to practical problems should broaden their educational background to include courses outside of physics, such as economics, computer technology, and current affairs.

Good oral and written communication skills are also important because many physicists work as part of a team or have contact with persons with nonphysics backgrounds, such as clients or customers.

The starting position for most physics and astronomy doctoral graduates is conducting research in a postdoctoral position, where they may work with experienced physicists as they continue to learn about their specialties and develop ideas and results to be used in later work.

Geologists and Geophysicists

A bachelor's degree in geology or geophysics is adequate for entry into some lower-level geology jobs, but better jobs with good advancement potential usually require at least a master's degree. Individuals with strong backgrounds in physics, chemistry, mathematics, or computer science also may qualify for some geophysics or geology jobs. A doctoral degree is required for most research positions in colleges and universities and is also important for work in federal agencies and some state geological surveys that involve basic research.

Hundreds of colleges and universities offer bachelor's degree programs in geology, geophysics, oceanography, or other geosciences. Other programs offering related training for beginning geological scientists include geophysical technology, geophysical engineering, geophysical prospecting, engineering geology, petroleum geology, hydrology, and geochemistry. In addition, several hundred universities award advanced degrees in geology or geophysics.

Traditional geoscience courses emphasizing classical geologic methods and topics (such as mineralogy, paleontology, stratigraphy, and structural geology) are important for all geoscientists. However, those students interested in working in the environmental or regulatory fields should take courses in hydrology, hazardous waste management, environmental legislation, chemistry, mechanics, and geologic logging. Also, some employers seek applicants with field experience, so a summer internship or employment in an environmentally related area may be beneficial to prospective geoscientists.

Geologists and geophysicists often begin their careers in field exploration or as research assistants in laboratories. They are given more difficult assignments as they gain experience. Eventually they may be promoted to project leaders, program managers, or other management or research positions.

Geologists and geophysicists need to be able to work as part of a team. Computer modeling, data processing, and effective oral and written communication skills are important, as well as the ability to think independently and creatively.

Meteorologists

A bachelor's degree with a major in meteorology (or a closely related field with course work in meteorology) is the usual minimum requirement for a beginning job as a meteorologist.

Although positions in operational meteorology are available for those who have earned a bachelor's degree, obtaining a graduate degree enhances advancement potential. A master's degree is usually necessary for conducting research and development, and a doctorate may be required for some research positions. Students who plan a career in research and development need not necessarily major in meteorology as an undergraduate. In fact, a bachelor's degree in mathematics, physics, or engineering is excellent preparation for graduate study in meteorology.

The federal government's National Weather Service is the largest employer of civilian meteorologists.

Because meteorology is a small field, relatively few colleges and universities offer degrees in meteorology or atmospheric science, although many departments of physics, earth science, geography, and geophysics offer atmospheric science and related courses. Prospective students should make certain that courses required by the National Weather Service and other employers are offered at the college they are considering. Computer science courses, additional meteorology courses, and a strong background in mathematics and physics are important to prospective employers. Many programs combine the study of meteorology with another field, such as agriculture, engineering, or physics. For example, *hydrometeorology* is the blending of hydrology (the science of the Earth's water) and meteorology and is the field concerned with the effect of precipitation on the hydrologic cycle and the environment. Beginning meteorologists often do routine data collection, computation, or analysis and some basic forecasting. Entry-level meteorologists in the federal government are usually placed in intern positions for training and experience. Experienced meteorologists may advance to various supervisory or administrative jobs or may handle more complex forecasting jobs. Increasing numbers of meteorologists establish their own weather consulting services.

Employment Outlook

Chemists

Employment of chemists is expected to grow about as fast as the average for all occupations. The chemical industry, the major employer of chemists, should face continued demand for goods, such as new and better pharmaceuticals and personal care products, as well as more specialty chemicals designed to address specific problems or applications. To meet these demands, research and development expenditures in the chemical industry will continue to increase, contributing to employment opportunities for chemists.

Within the chemical industry, job opportunities are expected to be most plentiful in pharmaceutical and biotechnology firms. Stronger competition among drug companies and an aging population are among the several factors contributing to the need for innovative and improved drugs discovered through scientific research. Although employment growth is expected to be slower in the remaining segments of the chemical industry, there will still be a need for chemists to develop and improve products, such as cosmetics and cleansers, as well as the technologies and processes used to produce chemicals for all purposes. Job growth will also be spurred by the need for chemists to monitor and measure air and water pollutants to ensure compliance with local, state, and federal environmental regulations.

Because much of the employment growth for chemists is expected to relate to drug research and development and environmental issues, analytical, environmental, and synthetic organic chemists should have the best job prospects.

Physicists and Astronomers

A large proportion of physicists and astronomers are employed on research projects, many of which, in the past, were defense related. Expected reductions in defense-related research and an expected slowdown in the growth of civilian physics-related research will cause employment of physicists and astronomers to decline. Proposed employment cutbacks and overall budget tightening in the federal government will also affect employment of physicists, especially those dependent on federal research grants. In addition, the number of doctorates granted in physics has been much greater than the number of openings for physicists for several years. Although physics enrollments are starting to decline slightly, the number of new doctoral graduates is likely to continue to be high enough to result in keen competition for the kind of research and academic jobs that those with new doctorates in physics have traditionally sought. Also, more prospective researchers will likely compete for less grant money.

Although research and development budgets in private industry will continue to grow, many research laboratories in private industry are expected to reduce basic research, which is where much physics research takes place, in favor of applied or manufacturing research and product and software development. Furthermore, although the median age of physicists and astronomers is higher than the average for all occupations and many will be eligible for retirement in the next decade, it is possible that many of them will not be replaced when they retire.

Geologists and Geophysicists

Many jobs for geologists and geophysicists are within, or related to, the petroleum industry (especially the exploration for oil and gas), and, unfortunately, this industry is subject to cyclical fluctuations. Low oil prices, higher production costs, improvements in energy efficiency, shrinking oil reserves, and restrictions on potential drilling sites have caused exploration activities to be curtailed in the United States. If these conditions continue, there will be limited openings in the petroleum industry for geoscientists working in the United States.

Despite the generally poor job prospects encountered by geoscientists in recent years in the petroleum industry, employment of geologists and geophysicists is expected to grow as fast as the average for all occupations. Recent setbacks have been offset by increased demand for these professionals in environmental protection and reclamation. Geologists and geophysicists will continue to be needed to help clean up contaminated sites in the United States and to help private companies and government comply with more numerous and complex environmental regulations. In particular, jobs requiring training in engineering geology, hydrology, and geochemistry should be in demand. However, the number of geoscientists obtaining training in these areas has been increasing, so they may experience competition despite the increasing number of jobs available.

Meteorologists

Prospective meteorologists may face competition if the number of degrees awarded in atmospheric science and meteorology remain near current levels, coupled with projected slower-than-average employment growth. The National Weather Service

(NWS) recently completed an extensive modernization of its weather forecasting equipment and all hiring of meteorologists needed to staff the upgraded stations. The NWS has no plans to increase the number of weather stations or the number of meteorologists in existing stations for many years.

There will continue to be demand for meteorologists to analyze and monitor the dispersion of pollutants into the air to ensure compliance with the federal environmental regulations outlined in the Clean Air Act of 1990.

Earnings

According to the United States Bureau of Labor Statistics, the average yearly salary for chemists is $49,510. The most recent figures offered by the U.S. Bureau of Labor Statistics list $52,480 as the average yearly salary for physical scientists.

The Bureau's most recent survey lists an average yearly salary for geologists and geophysicists as $57,210 and $52,480 for meteorologists.

Parade of Professionals

Sara Sawtelle, Ph.D., Chemist

Dr. Sawtelle serves as the manager of technical services at Environmental Test Systems in Elkhart, Indiana. ETS was founded in 1985 to develop consumer and industrial applications for reagent strip technology. Test strips have been widely used in the medical diagnostic industry since the 1960s, when their introduction revolutionized the way physicians performed urinalysis and blood tests. The company has adapted the technology for applications in such diverse fields as pool and spa water testing, drinking water quality testing, automobile and diesel truck coolant testing, and industrial in-process testing. Research and development efforts are ongoing as scientists continuously explore a variety of potential applications for the test strip.

"I was attracted to chemistry because of all the interesting things that are part of chemistry," Dr. Sawtelle recalls. "The more I learned, the more intrigued I became with how chemistry and life were connected. So I pursued an education focused in science. I earned my B.S. in chemistry from Clarion University of Pennsylvania in 1988. Subsequently, I earned my Ph.D. in analytical chemistry from Boston College in Chestnut Hill, Massachusetts, in 1992.

"I started here on May 12, 1997. Environmental Test Systems was looking for a chemist with good communication and people skills. At the time, I was teaching at a local college while seeking an area position that would let me make use of the parts of teaching that I enjoy, while omitting the parts I did not. This position does just that!

"My job does not have a typical day," says Dr. Sawtelle. "I am very busy but not over stressed. I work forty-plus hours per week in an atmosphere that is very team oriented. As a member of technical services, I am a part of the marketing department. This enables me to share the joy of chemistry with others, particularly nonchemists. I find the interactions intriguing and usually come away learning more all the time. It is also an environment that encourages out-of-the-box thinking—one in which we are encouraged to grow and learn. I assist customers with technical questions, acting as the technical liaison between the lab and the marketing department. I spend time talking with customers about our products, learn about new products that are coming out, and help in the legwork of marketing and developing a new product.

"I really enjoy working in this environment. The strength of this company is that from the president down to the line worker, everyone is considered important and has an invaluable function. It is a nice atmosphere in which to thrive.

"The most difficult part of the job is working with difficult customers. But this is to be expected. Still, the hard part is not letting them get to you so that you join them in their attitude.

"Most of my job centers around communication—communication within the company, communication between scientists and nonscientists, communication externally with customers explaining problems to them in lay terms. Communication is also of the utmost importance in presentations, which are given to professionals who use our products in the field.

"My previous experience of five years of teaching chemistry at the college level has been very valuable in this undertaking. Among other things, it taught me how to listen and not jump to conclusions about what a person may be asking.

"My advice to others interested in this field is to believe in yourself and to not try to be someone else. Don't try to change who you are. And don't expect that the job you get out of college or school to be 'the job' for you. As you grow as a person, be willing to try new things or new career paths. I never thought I would be where I am. I expected to become a college professor. But once I tried it, I found that there were aspects of that profession that did not work for me. I like being in the position I am in. So I guess my advice is to make sure you like your career, or it is just not worth your energy. If you don't like it, move on."

Kevin T. M. Johnson, Ph.D., Research Geologist

Dr. Johnson is employed by both the Bishop Museum and the University of Hawaii in Honolulu.

"I was always interested in oceans and volcanoes, and my choice of marine geology seemed natural," says Dr. Johnson.

"Both of my parents introduced me to and encouraged me in science and academic achievement. This probably had the biggest bearing on my career—everything followed from that.

"I earned a B.S. from Penn State, an M.S. from the University of Hawaii, and my Ph.D. from MIT and Woods Hole Oceanographic Institute. Subsequently, I served as a research fellow at the University of Tokyo.

"My job is quite varied," he says. "I spend about 75 to 80 percent of my time doing basic marine geological research on projects that I have received external funding to carry out. Most of my research funding is from the National Science Foundation. Primarily, my projects deal with the formation of ocean basins and oceanic crust at mid-ocean ridges and oceanic islands. I spend months at sea each year on research expeditions collecting samples and data, then I analyze the samples and data back on land. In addition to this, I collaborate with archaeologists in studies of stone tools and secure funding from smaller agencies and contractors to carry out more specific, applied research.

"I also give public lectures on volcanoes, geology, and earth sciences and also lead field trips to Kilauea, the active volcano on the island of Hawaii. In addition, I advise museum exhibits staff on technical matters within my area of knowledge, in addition to fielding questions from the public. So I am very busy day to day and spend about sixty to seventy hours per week on the various aspects of my job. The work atmosphere at both the museum and the university is quite pleasant, and I enjoy the interactions I have with my colleagues and students.

"I truly enjoy research because it allows me to pursue questions of my own choosing and to interact with interesting and intelligent people, both colleagues and students. Also, since I don't have to punch a time clock, doing research gives me a lot of time flexibility and a relaxed schedule. The part I enjoy least is the process of research proposal writing because it takes a considerable amount of time to write a good proposal, and the competition for funds is very keen.

"I would advise others to be very studious in school and in life in general. Enjoy the world around you and be inquisitive about the natural phenomena you observe every day. Ask questions and think about possible answers."

Charles L. Dumoulin, Ph.D., Research Scientist

Dr. Dumoulin serves as a physicist in the field of medicine. He has been on staff at General Electric's Research and Development Center in Schenectady, New York, since 1984. In 1996, he received the center's highest honor, its Coolidge Fellowship Award, which recognizes sustained contribution to science or engineering. Dr. Dumoulin was honored for his pioneering contributions to magnetic resonance imaging (MRI). He has published eighty-three peer-reviewed papers and twenty-four chapters in books, has obtained sixty-one issued patents, and has eleven patents pending.

"Although I was always fascinated by science as a child (and high school showed me I had a knack for science and math)," says Dr. Dumoulin, "my original career plan was to become a military officer. When I learned that my eyesight was too poor, I changed my plans and went to Florida State University, choosing chemistry as my major. After school and during summer vacations, I worked in a television and appliance repair shop and realized that I enjoyed learning how things work (televisions, radios, washing machines, refrigerators, and so forth). I also learned that the best way to understand something was to take it apart, fix it, and put it back together. I found solving problems to be most enjoyable. As I became a researcher, I found that the most fun problems to tackle were those that required creative solutions and addressed real-life problems. I also found that, unlike many fields, science generally dealt with questions that have objective and provable answers.

"Subsequently, I earned a Ph.D. from Florida State University in analytical chemistry in 1981. After I received my Ph.D., I moved with my thesis professor to Syracuse University, where I became a nontenure-track assistant professor. For three years I helped run a lab, did some research, and was cofounder of a small company. I came to realize, however, that this environment was not allowing me to develop as a researcher.

"I then moved to GE's Research and Development Center, where I changed my focus from nuclear magnetic resonance spectroscopy for chemistry to the related topic of magnetic resonance (MR) for medical applications.

"For the last thirteen years I have been working as a physicist in the field of medicine. I have worked primarily to develop new ways to perform diagnostic and interventional procedures with magnetic resonance imaging (MRI) scanners. Major projects which I have led, or been a part of, include MR spectroscopy, MR angiography (use of radio frequency signals to follow devices in real time), MR measurements of kidney function, MR tracking of interventional devices in real time, cardiac MR imaging, and use of MR to increase basic understanding of flow physiology in blood vessels.

"Although I'm paid to work forty hours per week, I typically work eight to nine hours per day and frequently a few hours during the weekend. Even when I'm not working, I often find myself thinking about problems at work. Some of my most productive moments occur while trying to fall to sleep and driving to or from work.

"As a scientist working in industry, my job is somewhat different than that of an academic scientist working in a university. For example, I have to justify my work as having some relevance to my company. Consequently, most of what I do can be called *applied science* rather than *basic science*.

"The work atmosphere here is relatively relaxed, yet there is always a certain intensity of purpose. I am surrounded by extremely capable colleagues who have been trained in a number of different scientific disciplines (such as computer science, physical chemistry, physics, astrophysics, medicine, electrical engineering). We tend to work in ad hoc teams, and conflicts are rare. Every Friday we meet to discuss topics as diverse as life in the universe, politics, or even 'Dilbert.'

"A nice aspect of my job is that every day brings unique challenges and tasks. A typical day begins with the reading and answering of E-mail. I interact with many people in Europe and Japan, and we have found that E-mail is the best way to communicate. One or two days each week I sign up to use the MRI scanner in our building. I spend those days testing new ideas and performing experiments. When I'm not in the lab, I can usually be found at my desk writing (E-mail, memos, papers, and so forth), or in meetings with my colleagues.

"My job frequently requires me to travel. My trips often take me to conferences where I speak about my work and listen to other scientists speak about theirs. I find that these talks are often a great source of inspiration. Other trips take me to different research hospitals around the world where I work with doctors to develop and evaluate new ways of using MRI scanners.

"To me the best part of this career is the intellectual challenge of finding creative solutions to problems—the exposure to new ideas within and beyond my profession and working on medical diagnostic methods that have direct relevance to patients. I also enjoy the latitude I have to define my own research agenda (although I wish I had more), working with some of the best scientists and engineers in the world, and the opportunity to talk to students of all ages about science and technology.

"I'd recommend to all prospective scientists that you remain as broad as possible. Scientific success often occurs by the synergistic combination of two or more existing ideas from different disciplines.

"It's important to stay focused on competing projects. But somehow you must concentrate on each project at every stage of its being. And usually a project is not considered complete until a publication (such as a memo, paper, patent application, and so forth) is submitted.

"It is always in your best interests to use the golden rule when dealing with everyone. Be particularly sensitive to the issue of sharing credit with your coworkers. Virtually all discoveries are accomplished as a result of the efforts of many—be sure everyone gets his or her just portion of the rewards!"

James L. Erjavec, Environmental Geologist

James L. Erjavec earned a B.S. in geology from Cleveland State University in Ohio and an M.S. in economic geology from the University of Arizona in Tucson. Presently, he is employed by Parsons Infrastructure and Technology in Cincinnati, Ohio.

"What attracted me to geology is that it is a field that incorporates almost all of the other sciences—chemistry, astronomy, biology, and so on," says Erjavec. "Furthermore, geology and the earth were always of interest to me, even as far back as when I was a child collecting fossils from stream cuts. As I grew up, the more I read about the Earth, the more fascinated I became. Geology had become a passion. When I entered college, I already knew that it was the field I wanted to study. Everything we are and everything we do relates to geology in some manner. I felt that not only as a career, but also as a fulfillment of my goals, the study of geology would open my eyes to the wonders and mysteries of our planet. So far I have not been wrong.

"My first job in the field was with Texaco in Los Angeles, California. I hired on with Texaco right out of graduate school in 1981. At the time, a geologist could easily find employment in the oil industry. My degree was more related to mining and mineral resources, and I made attempts to find work in those areas, but such jobs were scarce and difficult to obtain. The training I required to convert from 'hard' rock to 'soft' rock geology was obtained through Texaco.

"In 1985, the state of the petroleum industry changed from good times to bad. Massive layoffs were occurring in many companies. It was at that time I realized that just having a degree in geology was not enough to warrant continued employment. We had incorporated computer systems into our exploration program in 1983. However, as a newcomer to mainframe computers, I was flustered by their complexity. I marveled at a coworker who was an expert in using these systems. One day I asked him how he became so proficient.

"Laughing at me, as if I had given him praise he didn't deserve, he told me bluntly, 'Keep working at it. Don't be afraid to try things. The more you use computers, the more you'll understand them. Eventually, it will become so familiar to you that you'll think nothing of what I'm doing.' I took his advice seriously and in time I found myself doing all of my work on the computer. Then the day came when I realized what he had told me. I had passed some magical gate and actually understood what it was I was doing and the entire chain of logic that enabled me to do it. My acquired confidence and skills didn't go unnoticed. I was promoted to the computer systems group and began training others in the use of the systems. Within a year, though, the Texaco oil wells went dry. Layoffs occurred and I, along with hundreds of others, was out of work.

"However, because I now had extensive computer knowledge, I was able to switch careers and obtain a job with Intergraph Corporation, the vendor that Texaco bought its systems from. Though the work was not closely tied to geology, I enjoyed the challenge of a new field. I gained as much knowledge as I could while working at Intergraph as the company migrated from DEC/VAX mainframes to Unix workstations and finally to personal computers. My change of career fields paid off when I moved back into a geology role with Parsons, using my combination of computer and geology experience to my advantage.

"My job is a combination of challenging projects and routine tasks. Normally I work with computers every day, all day. The work involves the analysis and graphical depiction of subsurface and surface data that is used to guide many of the cleanup and restoration operations at the Fernald Environmental Management Project in southwest Ohio, a site of uranium contamination. I work closely with engineering groups who design and implement the processes for contaminant removal and environmental restoration. Using Geographic Information System technologies, I develop maps, cross sections, terrain models, contaminant plume models, and calculated datasets, as well as assist with a wide variety of activities that occur at the site. Fieldwork occurs on occasion and geology is often part of my work. The work week is normally forty hours and the atmosphere relaxed. But because deadlines dictated by the EPA and DOE must be met, some months become hectic.

"What I like most about the work is that I am able to use my geology education in this position. Also, the work is often challenging and thought provoking. It is also the type of work where new and innovative ideas are needed to keep things moving. The types of jobs I work on vary considerably. The downside is that work is often sporadic in nature because of government schedules. Some months are extremely busy—everyone seems to need something done for his or her particular operation—while other months are not as busy.

"My advice to others would be to focus on staying self-motivated. Realize that a college degree does not guarantee employment in your area of study. Be flexible and willing to see opportunities for growth as you mature in your working career. Gain as much knowledge and skills in other areas as you can. This will give you more success in staying employed and will allow you to change career fields if you desire (or need to). And to reiterate—be self-motivated."

For More Information

For a pamphlet on careers in astronomy, send your request to:

American Astronomical Society
Education Office
Adler Planetarium and Astronomy Museum
1300 South Lake Shore Drive
Chicago, IL 60605
http://www.aas.org

General information on career opportunities and earnings for chemists is available from:

American Chemical Society
Education Division
1155 Sixteenth Street NW
Washington, DC 20036

Information on training and career opportunities for geologists is available from:

American Geological Institute
4220 King Street
Alexandria, VA 22302
http://www.agiweb.org

Geological Society of America
P.O. Box 9140
Boulder, CO 80301
http://www.geosociety.org

American Association of Petroleum Geologists
Communications Department
P.O. Box 979
Tulsa, OK 74101

Information on training and career opportunities for geophysicists is available from:

American Geophysical Union
2000 Florida Avenue NW
Washington, DC 20009

Information on meteorology careers is available from:

American Meteorological Society
45 Beacon Street
Boston, MA 02108
http://www.ametsoc.org/AMS

A list of education and training and career programs in oceanography and related fields is available from:

Marine Technology Society
1828 L Street NW, Suite 906
Washington, DC 20036

General information on career opportunities in physics is available from:

American Institute of Physics
Career Planning and Placement
One Physics Ellipse
College Park, MD 20740

The American Physical Society
Education Department
One Physics Ellipse
College Park, MD 20740
http://ww.aps.org

Information on acquiring a job as a chemist, geologist, geophysicist, hydrologist, meteorologist, or oceanographer with the federal government may be obtained from the Office of Personnel Management through a telephone-based system. Consult your telephone directory under U.S. Government for a local number. Information also is available on the Internet at http://www.usajobs.opm.gov.

CHAPTER FIVE

Careers in the World of Invention

A man likes marvelous things; so he invents them, and is astonished. EDGAR WATSON HOWE

> ## Help Wanted—Inventor
> The Research and Development team in our major plastics manufacturing corporation needs an extraordinarily creative thinker to help develop new products. You would have engineering, production, and support staff at your disposal to create working prototypes to your specifications. We are looking for someone whose trach record includes several U.S. patents but who has ideas and drive to pursue even more as part of our team. Pay is commensurate with education and experience, although ideas and proven inventive abilities are priorities for obtaining the position. Excellent benefits package and bonuses for successful ventures. Send resume and copies of at least two previous patents.

Were you the kind of person who was always devising a better way to do something or build something—a faster toy car, a better-sounding radio, a more efficient mousetrap? Maybe you were destined to become an inventor. Take the following quiz and you might gain some insights.

1. Have you always enjoyed taking things apart (and hopefully putting them back together)?

2. Do you often find that you have a better way to do something?

3. Do you like to systematically draw or sketch ideas?

4. Are you an innovator?

5. Do you like working on your own?

6. Can you withstand disappointment when things don't work out as planned?

7. Are you a dreamer of new ideas, concepts, and so forth?

8. Are you self-motivated?

9. Do you follow through on things on your own?

If you answered "yes" to the majority of these questions, then you're probably an inventive type.

Welcome to the World of Inventing

Inventors dedicate their lives to creating something where there once was nothing. They may have some idea of what path to follow, but they really don't know if their choices will take them where they want to go. Unlike other people, they just can't go through life making use of things in the usual way. They are compelled to take things apart, ponder upon what they see, and contemplate ways that things could work better. Inventors just can't resist the urge to explore their environment by "playing" with the things around them.

Basically there are two types of inventors—those who work for themselves and those who work for someone else. Though it's true that the greater number, and more complex, of inventions are made by the research and development departments at large corporations, universities, and governmental agencies, independent inventors are still out there—creating and improving on what already exists, obtaining patents, and bringing their new concepts to the public.

However, anyone who is interested in becoming a freelance inventor should seriously consider the benefits of working for someone else, at least initially. Inventors who work for other people have many advantages over those who work for themselves. They gain valuable knowledge about procedures, systems of thinking, and how modern inventing works, and they may even gain important contacts. They are usually allowed to work with larger, more expensive equipment. They don't have to do as much to get their products to the public, and they get a steady paycheck. On the other hand, they rarely get to keep the rights to the things they invent, they don't have much control over the future of their creations, and they continue to get the same steady paycheck—even if they just made a billion dollars for their employers!

An independent inventor may do some contract research and development on the side while some employed inventors may be working on personal projects in their own basements.

While independent inventors focus on just about any area—from the simple to the very complex—they tend to invent the smaller, less expensive devices and gadgets that most of us have in our homes, such as paper clips, potato peelers, and pencil sharpeners. Those may all be simple inventions, but they make our lives much easier.

Invention, Innovation, and Discovery

People often use *invention, innovation,* and *discovery* synonymously, but actually there are distinct differences between them. An invention is something brand new. Even though some of the parts of the invention may not be based on original ideas, the finished product must become something that is totally new.

Innovation is far more common than invention. An innovation improves on an already existing process or product, but nothing new is created.

Discovery can happen as a planned event or a total accident of luck. For example, Benjamin Franklin is generally credited with discovering electricity. Actually, he really didn't, but he was the first to perform a major experiment with it and the first to discover its properties. In fact, he provided us with most of what we know about electricity—even to this day. But there is no invention involved here—simply a huge discovery based upon observation.

Education and Training

Though there is no clear-cut path to becoming an inventor, here are some suggestions to lead you toward that career. Learn everything you can about inventing, including its history and its modern applications and routines. Read some biographies about famous inventors. Try to figure out what common traits inventors have. Do you see those traits in yourself? There are many good books on inventing that take you through the process step by step, from getting your idea down on paper to making a prototype to getting a patent to finding funding to negotiating a deal with a manufacturer.

Becoming a successful inventor requires a solid education because in order to improve things in the world, you need to know how they work now. Choose the area that interests you, major in that, and gain internships. All inventors should know a lot about at least one area and a little about everything else. Everything doesn't have to be learned in a classroom. Read books and magazines on a wide variety of topics. Journals such as *Discover* or *Scientific American* are particularly beneficial. Attend workshops geared to inventors that are offered in your area.

Observe the world around you. How can things be improved? Where do you see that things are lacking? What items would make life easier for most of us? How can you make a contribution to society? Dream your dreams. Research areas that are relevant. Jot things down. Explore. Compare. Contrast. Imagine.

Analytical skills are essential to being successful as an inventor. The best way to improve these skills is to sign up for science classes because analysis is an important part of every class. Other good classes to foster this are history, philosophy, and English. History encourages you to identify and analyze why things happened the way they did. English is important because it teaches you how to organize your thoughts and then how to express them in an understandable and efficient way. These skills become important when you fill out applications at the U.S. Patent Office or when you are in need of funding and you must write proposals to solicit funds.

Other courses that are particularly beneficial include psychology, fine and applied arts, political science, marketing, business administration, and law.

As ideas come to you—or snippets of ideas or solutions to problems—start a filing system so that you can easily refer to and, when the time comes, organize your ideas so that you can proceed.

When you think you have come up with an idea, try it out! Does it seem feasible? Does it work physically? How does it need to be adjusted? Do you know how to accomplish these refinements? Always challenge yourself to come up with something even better. Plant the seeds of creative new ideas in your mind and see what sprouts from there. Don't forget that all inventors build on what exists already, taking up where the last inventors left off.

Inventors—particularly independent inventors—must have a fertile imagination, persistence, discipline, tenacity, an outstanding work ethic, and the ability to be productive, happy, and successful. Don't think of your inventing as a hobby—take it seriously. The work ethic is what separates successful inventors from those who merely tinkerers. There are no shortcuts to success.

How It Works

For a first invention, start with something simple. Then locate one of the seventy-two patent depository libraries that are located throughout the country to make sure that you don't duplicate someone else's idea. Each of these libraries maintains a complete listing of all patents previously granted.

Once you come up with an idea, you will need to build a prototype—a first example of your product. If your product is a simple household gadget, you can probably build it yourself. If it is something large and complex, you will need help to make it a reality. Banks are the usual source of financing. Alternatives to banks are venture capitalists, people or organizations that provide funding, or capital, for new business ideas. They can be easier to win over than banks, but they will want to be "cut in" as a return on their money. Banks lend you money and expect to be paid back with interest, whereas venture capitalists lend you money in exchange for a percentage of the profits.

It is smart to at least apply for a patent before showing your creation to any potential manufacturer, but you are safe discussing your ideas with a reputable attorney. If you do consult a patent attorney, the initial fee will be in the range of $500 to $1,000. The complete costs of securing a patent will begin at about $5,000 (including attorney fees). Patent attorneys will assist with the process of patenting your product and protecting it from powerful business predators who might try to take unfair advantage of you and your idea.

Independents can either license their inventions to a manufacturer or set up their own company and make an attempt to market their inventions. With a licensing agreement, the inventor receives a percentage royalty based upon the number of items sold by the manufacturer. To start your own company, you have to raise capital and have the management resources to produce the item. You may or may not make a profit, depending upon how successful sales are and how efficiently you operate the business.

The process of getting an invention into the marketplace can take a long time. In fact, it takes an average of two years to completely negotiate the process for most inventions, and this is only if the idea is an exceptionally good one. Most go back to the drawing board many times before manufacturing begins in earnest, meaning that it still takes a year or two to get your idea into production even after you have managed to elicit interest from manufacturers.

Employment Outlook

It's difficult to judge the employment outlook for inventors. However, we know that we live in a world that is constantly looking for new and innovative products and services. We know, also, that large companies, governmental agencies, and universities will always have people working on research and development in order to feed this interest. In addition, there will always be independent inventors with foresight enough to see new and exciting products that will benefit people all over the world.

Earnings

Earnings for inventors can range from nothing to unlimited figures. Inventors employed in full-time research and development usually receive regular salaries (that are usually quite good), but inventors who are employed by others will never earn millions. Independent inventors have it tough when it comes to making a living. Only a small number actually make a substantial amount of money from their inventions. However, at the other end of the scale, many of the world's billionaires (about five hundred worldwide) are inventors. They may not be inventing now, but they achieved these high income levels by having invented something.

Parade of Professionals

Gordon Matthews, Inventor

Credited with more than forty-five patents, Gordon Matthews is best known as the inventor of voice mail. In recognition of his industry contributions, he has received the Inventor of the Year Award from the Texas Bar Association and an Industry Achievement Award from the International Communications Association. He has also been nominated for induction into the National Inventor's Hall of Fame.

Matthews earned his B.S. in engineering physics from the University of Tulsa in Oklahoma. He began his career as an engineer in 1962, first with IBM and later with Texas Instruments, where he managed the development of the first minicomputer-based message switching system. In 1969, he founded his first company, Computer Control Systems, where he introduced a store-and-forward switching system used in the brokerage industry. A year later, he founded Action Communication Systems, where he managed the development of two products, the Tele-controller and the WATSBOX. The latter became the forerunner of today's computer-driven telephone systems.

In 1976, Matthews founded VMX to develop the first commercial voice messaging system. He sold the first system to the 3M company and played an integral part in all subsequent sales and marketing. During this time, he also oversaw the intellectual property of the enterprise, resulting in the granting of the pioneer patent for voice mail.

When Matthews recognized the need for call management systems for the burgeoning small office, home office (SOHO), and consumer markets, he founded Matthews Communications, now PremiseNET, in 1996. The company is based in Richardson, Texas. Today, as chairman of the board, he remains closely involved in the company's research and development efforts.

"I consider my profession to really be that of an entrepreneur and inventor," says Matthews. "I realized years ago that my unique talent was to create solutions to problems that impacted many people. My entrepreneurial ability was to create companies and products that could be made profitably and create solutions and shareholder value to the owners of the company.

"My first invention was an aircraft speech recognition system that would allow pilots to control cockpit functions, such as changing radio or navigational frequencies while flying formation or at night. This invention was in response to losing close friends who had been flying formation inside clouds.

"There is no typical day. I try to be sensitive to everyday problems around me that are looking for solutions. If there are large numbers of people with the same problem, and the system can be implemented with existing technology, then I try to create an environment whereby the problems are solved via products or services.

"In order to do this, it is better to work in an active environment, where I am exposed to many situations. Part of the responsibility of creation is to implement—therefore, significant time is spent in either taking the lead or assisting others in capital raising, team selection, product development, and product introduction.

"As far as the number of hours you spend, if you really enjoy what you are doing, you don't worry about the hours.

"The most rewarding part of my work is inventing products or services that enrich many people's lives. My work is so enjoyable to me that I can't think of a downside.

"I would advise others to make sure your real talent is to create and invent and that you have the ability to be a generalist while looking for a solution (invention). Once you have found it, you must be able to focus entirely on that opportunity until it is solved. How much more rewarding work could one do than to develop something that truly benefits humankind in some way? Go for it!"

For More Information

Affiliated Inventors Foundation
1405 Potter Drive, #107
Colorado Springs, CO 80909
http://www.affiliatedinventors.com

American Society of Patent Holders (Independent Inventors)
Inventive Place
221 South Broadway Street
Akron, Ohio 44308
http://www.invent.org/asph.html

Invent America!
P.O. Box 26065
Alexandria, VA 22313
http://www.inventamerica.org

United Inventors Association of the USA
P.O. Box 23447
Rochester, NY 14692
http://www.uiausa.com

CHAPTER SIX

Careers in Aeronautics

That's one small step for a man and one giant leap for mankind. NEIL ARMSTRONG

Help Wanted—Astronaut
Seeking individuals who want to serve their country and reach for the stars.
Please reply to NASA.

Welcome to the World of Astronauts

The space age began in the United States with the establishment of the National Aeronautics and Space Administration (NASA) in 1959. Created as a response to the launch of *Sputnik I* by the USSR, the agency's first goal was realized in 1969 when Neil Armstrong landed on the moon.

Though many Americans may consider space flights as almost routine, this is hardly the case. In 1967, Roger B. Chaffee, Edward White, and Virgil Ivan Grissom perished during the testing of the *Apollo I* rocket; the *Apollo 13* mission was a near tragedy; and the deaths of the astronauts aboard the *Challenger* spacecraft once again reminded all of us how dangerous space travel can be.

Though the word *astronaut* means "sailor among the stars," astronauts spend most of their time on the ground, preparing themselves to learn how to operate in space and gain knowledge of new horizons.

Blast Off!

Once astronauts are chosen and assigned to missions, they take their places as part of space shuttle crews, which consist of at least five people: the commander, the pilot, and three mission specialists, all of whom are NASA astronauts. Some flights also call for payload specialists, scientists or engineers responsible for the cargo being carried into space. Sometimes, engineers, technicians, physicians, meteorologists, or biologists are also included. Crew members are cross trained so that each one can handle at least one other associate's duties if necessary.

There are all kinds of jobs to do when you're in space. Here's what several crew members are expected to do on a mission.

Pilot astronauts are the commanders, or pilots, of the space shuttle. They are in charge of the vehicle, crew, and success of the mission. They maneuver the orbiter, supervise the crew and the operations of the vehicle, and are responsible for the safety of the flight. The commander and the second in command on the ship are both pilot astronauts who know how to fly aircraft and the spacecraft. Pilots help the commander control and operate the orbiter and may help manipulate satellites by using a remote control system. Like other crew members, they sometimes do work outside the craft or look after the payload.

Mission specialist astronauts work closely with the commander and pilot and are responsible for coordinating on-board operations involving crew activity planning, and overseeing payload activities. They are required to have a detailed knowledge of shuttle systems and are expected to perform experiments, space walks, and payload handling functions.

Payload specialists are skilled in operating shuttle equipment. Selection of this shuttle member is made by the payload sponsor or client and approved by NASA. A payload specialist receives intensive training for his or her mission assignment, such as launching a satellite into orbit, as well as comprehensive flight training to become familiar with the shuttle systems.

Astronauts in Action

While aboard the spacecraft, astronauts conduct a variety of experiments and other types of research under conditions of near-zero gravity. Laboratories may focus on or be related to earth sciences, astronomy, or manufacturing. Astronauts may also be in charge of deploying, servicing, or retrieving satellites or working with meters, sensors, special cameras, or other technical equipment. While in space, astronauts are able to increase our knowledge by observing the solar system and the earth, such as geological formations or pollution currents.

As with any career, being an astronaut has drawbacks. One commonly shared among astronauts is the lack of time for family because of the workload. Hours can be long and unpredictable. Travel is involved, especially during the busiest times—three months before and two months after a launch. A workday can last from 7:30 A.M. until 11:00 P.M. Also, most people would consider being an astronaut a high-risk occupation.

Education and Training

In high school, it's important for prospective astronauts to take engineering classes or advanced placement classes in math, biology, or physical science. English and a foreign language are also important. Since a career in space is one that extends internationally, knowing more than one language will help you communicate with astronauts from other countries.

Would-be candidates should also strive to earn high marks and score well on standardized tests (SAT and/or ACT). The minimum degree requirement is a bachelor's degree from an accredited institution. Also needed are three years of related professional experience. However, most astronauts have postgraduate degrees as well as considerable experience in their fields.

If you want to make sure you're taking the right courses in college, try to attend one of the fifty-one colleges and universities that are a part of the Space Grant Consortia. NASA contributes funds to these institutions to ensure they have a curriculum in line with NASA requirements. If you'd like a list of these colleges, you can write to:

NASA Education Division
Code FEO2
300 E Street SW
Washington, DC 20546

In order to gain vital experience, students should investigate the possibilities of internships or work-study positions. It would be wise to explore such career options early in your college career. Those who wait until the senior year could miss this valuable opportunity.

It is also important to know that if you want to be in a pilot or commander position on a space shuttle mission, you also have to have flight experience. In consideration of this important role, NASA requires at least one thousand hours of flight time in command of a jet aircraft.

Becoming a NASA Astronaut

Once you have finished the NASA requirements, you need to send in U.S. Government Application Form 171 to the Johnson Space Center in Houston, Texas. Your application will be ranked by physical considerations, such as height, experience, and expertise. Just like any other application process, you will be competing against many other candidates—an average of more than four thousand other applicants for about twenty slots that open up every two years. These applications continue to be narrowed down to the most qualified—usually around 120 applicants—

who then go through a week of interviews, medical exams, and orientation.

The Astronaut Selection Board (ASB) is particularly looking for people who have done very well in a technical field. Candidates should make sure that they have superior recommendations—especially from undergraduate and graduate school professors—that attest to your problem-solving abilities, communicability with others, and ability to work well in a team setting.

The ASB interviews each person and assigns them a rating based on experience and potential, motivation, ability to function as a member of a team, communicative abilities, and adaptability. Some applicants do not possess the required interpersonal skills and other requisite characteristics for the position and are rejected solely on that basis. A significant number of applicants do not meet medical standards, and still others withdraw after gaining a complete understanding of the job. Based on information collected during this investigation, ASB will choose its final candidates and pass those recommendations on to the NASA administrator, who will make the final selection. Once selected, candidates begin a rigorous training program.

Astronauts come from both military and civilian backgrounds. Pilots are chosen exclusively from a pool of high-achieving jet pilots who have accumulated more than one thousand hours of time in the air. Most pilot/commanders are individuals who have served or are currently serving in the armed forces. Civilian mission specialists are those with advanced training in areas such as astronomy, biology, medicine, or mathematics.

Candidates are selected from both civilian and military walks of life on a continuing basis as needed for the rigorous one-year training program directed by Johnson Space Center in Houston (JSC). Upon completing the course, successful candidates become regular members of the astronaut corps. Usually they become eligible for a flight assignment about one year after completing the basic training program.

Special Training for Astronauts

During training at the Johnson Space Center in Houston, Texas, astronauts must take further course work. In the formal academic areas, the novice astronauts are given a full range of basic science and technical courses, including mathematics, earth resources, meteorology, guidance and navigation, astronomy, physics, and computer sciences. They also spend time in weightless simulation drills learning how to conduct necessary work while wearing a space suit. Astronaut training is highly specialized and requires the efforts of literally hundreds of persons and numerous facilities. It is conducted under the auspices of JSC's Mission Operations Directorate.

Initial training for new candidates consists of a series of short courses in aircraft safety, including instruction on ejection, parachute, and survival, to prepare them in the event their aircraft is disabled and they have to eject or make an emergency landing. Pilot and mission specialist astronauts are trained to fly T-38 high-performance jet aircraft, which are based at Ellington Field near JSC. Flying these aircraft, pilot astronauts are able to maintain their flying skills and mission specialists are able to become familiar with high-performance jets.

As manned space flight programs have become more sophisticated over the years, so too has the complex training process needed to meet the demands of operating the space shuttle.

Basic knowledge of the shuttle system, including payloads, is obtained through lectures, briefings, textbooks, and flight operations manuals. Future crew members are trained in orbiter habitability, routine housekeeping and maintenance, waste management and stowage, television operations, and extravehicular activities.

As training progresses, the student astronauts gain one-on-one experience in the single systems trainers (SSTs). SSTs contain computer databases with software, allowing students to interact with controls and displays like those of a shuttle crew station. Here they can develop work procedures and react to malfunction situations in a shuttle-like environment.

Astronauts in training receive needed instruction about weightlessness. Learning to function in a weightless environment is simulated in aircraft and in an enormous "neutral buoyancy" water tank at JSC.

Training reaches its peak a few weeks prior to the flight when flight crew and ground controllers go through the entire mission in a joint training exercise.

Job Settings for Astronauts

Pilot and mission astronauts work mainly at the Lyndon B. Johnson Space Center in Houston, Texas (JSC). Other NASA space centers include Ames Research Center, Moffett Field, California; Goddard Space Flight Center, Greenbelt, Maryland; George C. Marshall Space Flight Center, Huntsville, Alabama; John F. Kennedy Space Center, Kennedy Space Center, Florida; Langley Research Center, Hampton, Virginia; Lewis Research Center, Cleveland, Ohio; Stennis Space Center, Bay Saint Louis, Mississippi.

Earnings

Astronauts begin their salaries in accordance with the U.S. government pay scale at GS-11 or GS-12 (approximately $45,000 to $50,000) status and may elevate to a GS-15 rating (approximately $68,000 to $90,000).

Parade of Professionals

James Arthur Lovell, Jr., Astronaut

As a high school junior, James Arthur Lovell, Jr., launched a rocket with the help of a chemistry teacher and two friends. Though it rose only eighty feet in the air and was only partially successful, Lovell knew even then that he longed for a career in rocket science. True to his ambition, Lovell became a U.S. Navy test pilot and was chosen to be an astronaut in 1962. He served as module pilot for the *Apollo 8* mission (the first manned flight to orbit the moon) and as a member of the *Gemini 7* crew (in space for two weeks), and he worked with pilot Edwin "Buzz" Aldrin on *Gemini 12* and served as commander of *Apollo 13* in 1970. The *Apollo 13* mission was very nearly a disaster, when an explosion caused the shuttle to lose oxygen and power. For four days, the world waited and prayed that somehow the astronauts would make it back home safely.

The story of the *Apollo 13* mission was made into a movie (based upon Lovell's book, originally titled *Lost Moon*), with actor Tom Hanks playing the part of Lovell. To become familiar with the details, Hanks traveled to meet and fly with Lovell. "I tried to convey to him my feelings, my actions, my views, my goals, my inner being, so he could gain some insights and a perception of the character," explains Lovell.

"To tell you the truth, I would have worked for NASA for nothing," says Lovell. "It was such an amazing and interesting job. And I wasn't the only one who felt this way. So did most of the other astronauts and a lot of other people who worked for NASA. The attrition rate at the time was almost zero because no one wanted to leave. That's because the sense of achievement and satisfaction you receive as an astronaut for a job well done is incredible—pioneering new avenues, new vistas, seeing things for the first time. *Apollo 8* was an awe-inspiring flight because I (and my mission mates) were the first to see the far side of the moon. So it's obviously one of the great milestones of my career.

"I feel that, in order to become a successful astronaut, a candidate must have the following qualities: curiosity, the ability to handle stress, the facility to work well in team situations, the initiative to see problems and overcome them, sufficient training in a particular discipline, such as biology or engineering, and the ability to perform optimally with only five or six hours of sleep per night! It's also important to be goal oriented and persistent. You need to be the kind of person who is motivated to accomplish goals and be qualified and ready to enhance luck to make it work for you in the best way possible.

"No matter what, I feel NASA will continue its efforts because it has proven to be a viable, creative program. Funding will fluctuate up and down, and the numbers of people involved may vary, but it will always attract well-qualified individuals who are motivated to explore new worlds and share in the thrill of learning things we never knew before."

For More Information

For information about the U.S. Space Camp/Space Academy for students, adults, and teachers, write to:

U.S. Space Camp/Space Academy and Aviation Challenge
U.S. Space and Rocket Center
One Tranquility Base
Huntsville, AL 35807

For a wealth of information about NASA, educational and career opportunities, student employment opportunities, and job openings and application procedures, visit the NASA website at http://www.nasa.gov.

Another helpful website, sponsored by the ALLSTAR Network (Aeronautics Learning Laboratory for Science, Technology, and Research), provides information on educational opportunities in aeronautics. The Web address is http://www.allstar.fiu.edu.

CHAPTER SEVEN

Careers in Engineering

If it keeps up, man will atrophy all his limbs but the push-button finger. FRANK LLOYD WRIGHT

Help Wanted—Staff Engineer

Our company develops and markets innovative products for surgeons, such as sutures and ligatures.

In this role, you will assess new technologies and product opportunities. This will involve focusing on intellectual property, feasibility of approach, product safety, and technical alternatives. You'll oversee collaborations with external technology sources, lead the incorporation of new technologies, develop prototypes, and provide technical training for your work group.

To qualify, you must have a Ph.D. in engineering or physics and one to two years of product design and development experience, preferably with medical devices. Five years of experience in the assessment of intellectual property and technology or a degree in engineering (B.S. or M.S.) is also acceptable. A background in patent searching, claims comparison, and patent mapping, along with working knowledge of domestic and international patents is essential. Thorough knowledge of the product development process is a must. The successful candidate will also have strong presentation, communication, and interpersonal skills.

As a valued team member, you'll receive a competitive salary and great benefits, including medical/dental, a 401(k), a pension plan, and a comprehensive wellness program. Please apply directly on-line at our website.

Welcome to the World of Engineering

Engineers apply the theories and principles of science and mathematics to the economical solution of practical technical problems. Usually their work is the link between a scientific discovery and its commercial application. Engineers design machinery, products, systems, and processes for efficient and economical performance. They design industrial machinery and equipment for manufacturing defense-related goods and weapons systems for the armed forces; design, plan, and supervise the construction of buildings, highways, and rapid transit systems; and design and develop systems for control and automation of manufacturing, business, and management processes.

Engineers consider many factors in developing a new product. For example, in developing an industrial robot, they determine precisely what function it needs to perform; design and test the necessary components; fit them together in an integrated plan; and evaluate the design's overall effectiveness, cost, reliability, and safety. This process applies to products as diverse as chemicals, computers, gas turbines, helicopters, and toys.

In addition to design and development, many engineers work in testing, production, or maintenance. Here they may supervise production in factories, determine the causes of breakdowns, and test manufactured products to maintain quality. They also estimate the time and cost to complete projects. Some work in engineering management or in sales, where an engineering background enables them to discuss the technical aspects of a product and assist in planning its installation or use.

Engineers often use computers to simulate and test how a machine, structure, or system operates. Many engineers also use computer-aided design systems to produce and analyze designs. They spend a great deal of time writing reports and consulting with other engineers, as complex projects often require an interdisciplinary team of engineers. Supervisory engineers are responsible for major components or entire projects.

Most engineers specialize. More than twenty-five major specialties are recognized by professional societies, and within the major branches are numerous subdivisions. Structural, environmental, and transportation engineering, for example, are subdivisions of civil engineering. Engineers also may specialize in one industry, such as motor vehicles, or in one field of technology, such as propulsion or guidance systems.

Acoustical Engineers

Acoustical engineers are called in when a particular situation demands their expertise. An example of this would be to adapt a noisy printer that needs to be used in an office environment.

Aerospace Engineers

Aerospace engineers design, develop, test, and help manufacture commercial and military aircraft, missiles, and spacecraft. They develop new technologies for use in commercial aviation, defense systems, and space exploration, often specializing in areas such as structural design, guidance, navigation and control, instrumentation and communication, or production methods. They may also specialize in a particular type of aerospace product, such as commercial transports, helicopters, spacecraft, or rockets. Aerospace engineers may be experts in aerodynamics, propulsion, thermodynamics, structures, celestial mechanics, acoustics, or guidance and control systems.

Chemical Engineers

Chemical engineers apply the principles of chemistry and engineering to solve problems involving the production or use of chemicals. Most work in the production of chemicals and chemical products. They design equipment and develop processes for manufacturing chemicals, plan and test methods of manufacturing the products, and supervise production. Chemical engineers also work in other industries, such as electronics or aircraft manufacturing. Because their knowledge and duties cut across many fields, chemical engineers apply principles of chemistry, physics, mathematics, and mechanical and electrical engineering to their work. They frequently specialize in a particular operation, such as oxidation or polymerization. Others specialize in a particular area, such as pollution control or the production of a specific product, such as automotive plastics or chlorine bleach.

Civil Engineers

Civil engineers work in the oldest branch of engineering. They design and supervise the construction of roads, airports, tunnels, bridges, water supply and sewage systems, and buildings. Major specialties within civil engineering include structural, water resources, environmental, construction, transportation, and geotechnical engineering.

Many civil engineers hold supervisory or administrative positions, ranging from supervisor of a construction site to city engineer. Others may work in design, construction, research, and teaching.

Electrical and Electronics Engineers

Electrical and electronics engineers design, develop, test, and supervise the manufacture of electrical and electronic equipment. Electrical equipment includes power generating and transmission equipment used by electric utilities, electric motors, machinery controls, and lighting and wiring in buildings, automobiles, and aircraft. Electronic equipment includes radar, computer hardware, and communications and video equipment.

The specialties of electrical and electronics engineers include power generation, transmission, and distribution; communications; computer electronics; electrical equipment manufacturing; or a subdivision of these areas—industrial robot control systems or aviation electronics, for example. Electrical and electronics engineers design new products, write performance requirements, and develop maintenance schedules. They also test equipment, solve operating problems, and estimate the time and cost of engineering projects.

Industrial Engineers

Industrial engineers determine the most effective ways for an organization to use the basic factors of production—people, machines, materials, information, and energy—to make or process a product. Acting as the bridge between management and operation, they are more concerned with increasing productivity through the management of people, methods of business organization, and technology than are engineers in other specialties who generally work more with products or processes.

To solve organizational, production, and related problems most efficiently, industrial engineers carefully study the product and its requirements, design manufacturing and information systems, and use mathematical analysis methods, such as operations research, to meet those requirements. They develop management control systems to aid in financial planning and cost analysis, design production planning and control systems to coordinate activities and control product quality, and design or improve systems for the physical distribution of goods and services. Industrial engineers conduct surveys to find plant locations with the best combination of raw materials, transportation, and costs. They also develop wage and salary administration systems and job evaluation programs. Many industrial engineers move into management positions because the work is closely related.

Manufacturing Engineers

Manufacturing engineers are involved in design and building of equipment and tools and work with all aspects of manufacturing.

They are needed to determine what manufacturing equipment will be necessary and how existing equipment will have to be modified. They may also continue to be involved throughout the manufacturing process to maintain quality and efficiency.

Mechanical Engineers

Mechanical engineers plan and design tools, engines, machines, and other mechanical equipment. In addition, many design and develop power-producing machines, such as internal combustion engines, steam and gas turbines, and jet and rocket engines. Another responsibility might be to create and develop power-using machines, such as refrigeration and air-conditioning equipment, robots, machine tools, materials handling systems, and industrial production equipment.

The work of mechanical engineers varies by industry and function. Specialties include applied mechanics, design engineering, heat transfer, power plant engineering, pressure vessels and piping, and underwater technology. Mechanical engineering is the broadest engineering discipline, extending across many interdependent specialties. Mechanical engineers may work in production operations, maintenance, or technical sales. Many are administrators or managers.

Metallurgical, Ceramic, and Materials Engineers

Metallurgical, ceramic, and materials engineers develop new types of metal alloys, ceramics, composites, and other materials that meet special requirements. Examples are graphite golf club shafts that are light but stiff, ceramic tiles that protect the space shuttle from burning up during reentry, and the alloy turbine blades in a jet engine.

Most metallurgical engineers work in one of the three main branches of metallurgy—extractive or chemical, physical, and mechanical or process. *Extractive metallurgists* are concerned with removing metals from ores and refining and alloying them to obtain useful metal. *Physical metallurgists* study the nature, structure, and physical properties of metals and their alloys and methods of processing them into final products. *Mechanical metallurgists* develop and improve metalworking processes, such as casting, forging, rolling, and drawing.

Ceramic engineers develop new ceramic materials and methods for making ceramic materials into useful products. Ceramics include all nonmetallic, inorganic materials which require high temperatures in their processing. Ceramic engineers work on products as diverse as glassware, semiconductors, automobile and aircraft engine components, fiber-optic phone lines, tile, and electric power line insulators.

Materials engineers evaluate technical requirements and material specifications to develop materials that can be used, for example, to reduce the weight but not the strength of an object. They also evaluate materials and develop new materials, such as the composite materials now being used in "stealth" aircraft.

Mining Engineers

Mining engineers find, extract, and prepare metals and minerals for use by manufacturing industries. They design open pit and underground mines, supervise the construction of mine shafts and tunnels in underground operations, and devise methods for transporting minerals to processing plants. Mining engineers are responsible for the safe, economical, and environmentally sound operation of mines. Some mining engineers work with geologists and metallurgical engineers to locate and appraise potential ore deposits. Others develop new mining equipment or direct mineral processing operations to separate minerals from the dirt, rock, and other materials with which they are mixed. Mining engineers frequently specialize in the mining of one mineral or metal, such as coal or gold.

With increased emphasis on protecting the environment, many mining engineers work on solving problems related to land reclamation and water and air pollution.

Nuclear Engineers

Nuclear engineers conduct research on nuclear energy and radiation. They design, develop, monitor, and operate nuclear power plants used to generate electricity and power navy ships. They may work on the nuclear fuel cycle; fusion energy; the production, handling, and use of nuclear fuel; and the safe disposal of waste produced by nuclear energy. Some specialize in the development of nuclear weapons; others develop industrial and medical uses for radioactive materials, such as equipment to diagnose and treat medical problems.

Petroleum Engineers

Petroleum engineers are explorers who search for workable reservoirs containing oil or natural gas. When one is discovered, petroleum engineers work to achieve the maximum profitable recovery from the reservoir by determining and developing the most efficient production methods. Because only a small proportion of the oil and gas in a reservoir will flow out under natural forces, petroleum engineers develop and use various enhanced recovery methods. These include injecting water, chemicals, or steam into an oil reservoir to force more of the oil out and horizontal drilling or fracturing to connect more of a gas reservoir to a well. Since even the best methods in use today recover only a portion of the oil and gas in a reservoir, petroleum engineers work to find ways to increase this proportion.

Software Engineers

Software engineers are responsible for designing software that will run computers. This includes both the operating systems and all other software used with computers, from personal computers to massive mainframes.

Other Engineering Careers

Branches of engineering not covered in detail here include *architectural engineering* (design of a building's internal support structure), *biomedical engineering* (application of engineering to medical and physiological problems), *environmental engineering* (a growing discipline involved with identifying, solving, and alleviating environmental problems), and *marine engineering* (design and installation of ship machinery and propulsion systems). For information on these and other disciplines, as well as lists of colleges that offer engineering programs, contact:

The American Society for Engineering Education
1818 N Street NW, Suite 600
Washington, DC 20036
http://www.asee.org/precollege

Education and Training

A bachelor's degree in engineering from an accredited engineering program is usually required for beginning engineering jobs. College graduates with a degree in a physical science or mathematics may occasionally qualify for some engineering jobs, especially in engineering specialties in high demand.

Most engineering degrees are granted in branches such as electrical, mechanical, or civil engineering. However, engineers trained in one branch may work in another because professionals in every branch of engineering have knowledge and training that can be applied to many fields. Electrical and electronics engineers, for example, work in the medical, computer, missile guidance, and power distribution fields. This flexibility allows employers to meet staffing needs in new technologies and specialties where engineers are in short supply. It also allows engineers to shift to fields with better employment prospects or to ones that match their interests more closely.

In addition to the standard engineering degree, many colleges offer two- or four-year degrees in engineering technology. These programs prepare students for practical design and production work rather than for jobs that require more theoretical, scientific, and mathematical knowledge. Graduates of four-year technology programs may get jobs similar to those obtained by graduates with bachelor's degrees in engineering. Some employers regard them as having skills between those of a technician and an engineer.

Graduate training is essential for engineering faculty positions but is not required for the majority of entry-level engineering jobs. Many engineers obtain graduate degrees in engineering or business administration to learn new technology, broaden their education, and enhance promotion opportunities; others obtain law degrees and become attorneys. Many high-level executives in government and industry began their careers as engineers.

A large number of colleges and universities offer bachelor's degrees in engineering, and many offer bachelor's degrees in engineering technology, although not all are accredited programs. Although most institutions offer programs in the larger branches of engineering, only a few offer some of the smaller specialties. Programs of the same title may vary in content; for example, some emphasize industrial practices, preparing students for jobs in industry, while others are more theoretical and are better for students preparing to do graduate work. Therefore, students should investigate curricula and check accreditations carefully before selecting a college. Admission requirements for undergraduate engineering schools include advanced courses in high school mathematics and the physical sciences.

Bachelor's degree programs in engineering are typically designed to last four years, but many students find that it takes between four and five years to complete their studies. In a typical four-year college curriculum, the first two years are spent studying basic sciences (mathematics, physics, and chemistry), introductory engineering, and the humanities, social sciences, and English. In the last two years, most courses are in engineering, usually with a concentration in one branch. For example, the last two years of an aerospace program might include courses such as fluid mechanics, heat transfer, applied aerodynamics, analytical mechanics, flight vehicle design, trajectory dynamics, and aerospace propulsion systems. Some programs offer a general engineering curriculum; students then specialize in graduate school or on the job.

A few engineering schools and two-year colleges have agreements whereby the two-year college provides the initial engineering education, and the engineering school automatically admits students for their last two years. In addition, a few engineering schools have arrangements whereby a student spends three years in a liberal arts college studying pre-engineering subjects and two years in the engineering school and receives a bachelor's degree from each. Some colleges and universities offer five year master's degree programs.

Some five- or even six-year cooperative plans combine classroom study and practical work, permitting students to gain valuable experience and finance part of their education.

All fifty states and the District of Columbia require registration for engineers whose work may affect life, health, or property or who offer their services to the public. Registration generally requires a degree from an engineering program accredited by the Accreditation Board for Engineering and Technology, four years of relevant work experience, and successful completion of a state examination. Some states will not register people with degrees in engineering technology. Engineers may be registered in more than one state.

Beginning engineering graduates usually do routine work under the supervision of experienced engineers and, in larger companies, may also receive formal classroom or seminar-type training. As they gain knowledge and experience, they may be assigned more difficult tasks with greater independence to develop designs, solve problems, and make decisions. Engineers may become technical specialists or may supervise a staff or team of engineers and technicians. Some eventually become engineering managers or enter other managerial, management support, or sales jobs.

Engineers should be able to work as part of a team and should be creative, analytical, and detail oriented. In addition, engineers should be able to communicate well, both orally and in writing.

Employment Outlook

Employment opportunities in engineering are expected to be good through the year 2006 because employment is expected to increase about as fast as the average for all occupations, while the number of degrees granted in engineering may not increase as rapidly as employment.

Many of the jobs in engineering are related to national defense. Because defense expenditures have declined, employment growth and job outlook for engineers may not be as strong as in times when defense expenditures were increasing. However, graduating engineers will continue to be in demand for jobs in engineering and other areas, possibly even at the same time other engineers, especially defense-industry engineers, are being laid off.

Employers will rely on engineers to further increase productivity as they increase investment in plant and equipment to expand output of goods and services. In addition, competitive pressures and advancing technology will force companies to improve and update product designs more frequently. Finally, more engineers will be needed to improve deteriorating roads, bridges, water and pollution control systems, and other public facilities.

Only a relatively small proportion of engineers leave the profession each year. Despite this, more than 70 percent of all job openings will arise from replacement needs. A greater proportion of replacement openings is created by engineers who transfer to management, sales, or other professional specialty occupations than by those who leave the labor force.

Most industries are less likely to lay off engineers than other workers. Many engineers work on long-term research and development projects or in other activities that may continue even during recessions.

New computer-aided design systems have improved the design process, enabling engineers to produce or modify designs much more rapidly. Engineers now produce and analyze many more design variations before selecting a final one. However, this technology is not expected to limit employment opportunities.

It is important for engineers to continue their education throughout their careers because much of their value to their employers depend on their knowledge of the latest technology. The pace of technological change varies by engineering specialty and industry. Engineers in high-technology areas, such as advanced electronics, may find that technical knowledge can become obsolete rapidly. Even those who pursue continue education are vulnerable if the particular technology or product they have specialized in becomes obsolete.

Engineers who have not kept current in their fields may find themselves passed over for promotions and are vulnerable should layoffs occur. On the other hand, these high-technology areas are most likely to offer the greatest challenges, the most interesting work, and the highest salaries. Therefore, the choice of engineering specialty and employer involves an assessment not only of the potential rewards but also of the risk of technological obsolescence.

Earnings

The latest figures from the United States Department of Labor Statistics list the following yearly average salaries:

Safety Engineers	$53,170
Agricultural Engineers	$53,710
Industrial Engineers	$54,450
Mechanical Engineers	$54,550
Civil Engineers	$54,660
Mining Engineers	$54,970
Metallurgists and Metallurgical, Ceramic, and Materials Engineers	$57,000
Electrical and Electronic Engineers	$59,670
Computer Engineers	$59,850
Chemical Engineers	$61,240
Nuclear Engineers	$68,020
Petroleum Engineers	$70,090
All Other Engineers	$59,160

Parade of Professionals

Mary Shafer, Senior Aerospace Engineer

Mary Shafer is a NASA senior aerospace engineer at the premier installation for aeronautical flight research, the Dryden Flight Research Center. Located in the Mojave Desert at Edward's Air

Force Base in California, the center celebrated its fiftieth anniversary in 1996. Dryden has grown from an initial group of five engineers to a facility with more than 460 NASA government employees and about the same number of civilian contractor personnel. In addition to carrying out aeronautical research, the center also supports the space shuttle program as a primary and backup landing site and as a facility to test and validate design concepts and systems used in development and operation.

"As a high school senior in the early sixties, I attended a National Science Foundation course at UCLA between my junior and senior years," Shafer says. "The subject happened to be meteorology, but it gave me a chance to see that science and research provided a way to explain the world around me, which I felt was interesting and important. Then I got a summer job working for the U.S. Air Force, where I discovered I liked being near airplanes.

"I began my college career at UCLA as a chemistry major but later switched to engineering, spending subsequent summers working for NASA. I decided I truly wanted to focus my career on airplanes and flight research and was lucky in my quest. I encountered a number of exceptional people who were willing to educate me about aerodynamics and fluid mechanics.

"During the summers at NASA I began by reducing data, working with a ruler in engineering units, plotting the information on graph paper with orange carbon behind it. I wrote a couple of smaller programs that impressed everybody (because at that point few people could do that). The next year I progressed to writing computer-matrix manipulations designed to measure trial-time stability analysis during flight. That was really interesting because I started to understand the rules that governed how airplanes flew.

"I earned my bachelor's degree and came back and worked another summer writing quality programs for some of the engineers. Then I went back and got my master's degree. The next summer I was writing with engineers and even married one!

"I began working as a computer programmer writing follow-up programs for the X-24B, then worked for Lockheed on the FA certification of the L-1011. I moved on to McDonnell Douglas and McDonnell Aircraft, then worked on the F-4 airplane and the initial acceptance testing of the F-15. Then I accepted a position in the air force as a systems designer working on writing programs. Finally, I came back over to NASA and got a job as a controls engineer.

"My projects vary, but right now, in addition to a number of small flying qualities research projects, I'm working on one particular experiment called the aerospy. It is my responsibility to look at an airplane's various flying qualities to make sure that any modifications that are made are safe. We must fulfill our priority of being able to fly airplanes that are structurally sound.

"Most of my day is spent either talking with pilots, studying data on various computers, visiting the simulation area to see how the plane is flying, watching the input of our new ideas, or observing what the airplane looks like with the new lift, drag, or whatever the case may be. Then we put the results of our efforts in the simulator so that the pilots can fly the planes and determine if the 'real' planes will fly as we want them to. For example, we focus on issues such as: Are we going to have enough runway to take off? Are we going to have enough thrust? Will it go forward instead of falling out of the sky?

"My other real interest lies in how the aircraft pilot system works and what the pilot needs to get from the airplane in order to feel that it's a good airplane or a bad airplane. In his opening sentence in *Anna Karenina*, Tolstoy says 'All happy families are alike, but each unhappy family is unhappy in its own way'. Well, the same is true of airplanes—a good airplane is not very interesting to a quality engineer, but a bad airplane is fascinating.

"I work fairly regular hours," says Shafer. "However, it's my understanding that this is somewhat less common in the university setting. The situation here is that we'll occasionally have a surge of work. For instance, I've got to write a paper that is due in three months, so I'll probably do that on weekends but then go back to a normal work schedule.

"NASA employs aeronautical engineers, mechanical engineers, electrical engineers, meteorologists, and physicists. We cover a broad range of disciplines: engineering and the hard sciences, chemistry, physics, meteorology, and math. It's important that you know math and extremely important that you know how to program and use the computer. Also, you need to know how to write with clarity and grammatical precision. There's no point in doing research if you can't write it down clearly and well enough that people can understand what you did, how you did it, why you did it, and what happened when you did it.

"Flexibility is another important quality for researchers because you don't know how your attempts are going to come out, and you have to be able to build upon your successes or shift gears when the outcome isn't as you planned. People who are unable to deal with uncertainty may find that research is not a good field for them. And in this line of work, a robust ego is a nice thing to have.

"Research is essentially a mutual endeavor. When you begin a project, you never really know what will be gained from your efforts, what will be gleaned, or how the new information might be used. It is only in the later stages of your work that you may be able to ascertain exactly how the information gained from your research will affect others on a grander scale. This is what provides fulfillment for all scientists and engineers—discovering information that can benefit the world in which we live."

Ernestine Meyers,
Senior Environmental Engineer

Ernestine Meyers serves as senior environmental engineer for the Division of Sanitation Facilities Construction in the Office of Environmental Health and Engineering of the U.S. Public Health Service in Albuquerque, New Mexico.

"While I was growing up, my summers were spent out in the field with my father," Meyers explains. "That's how I became familiar with inner workings of the Indian Health Service. He worked for the agency as an environmental health technician for thirty-two years. Together we would travel to different reservations, where I would observe what he did. I met and talked with engineers and got to know what they were responsible for. And, of course, I helped whenever I could. With my father as a role model and a love for science and the outdoors, I found my career direction.

"Born on a New Mexico pueblo reservation, I am the oldest of four children. Given my choice to attend the Bureau of Indian Affairs (BIA) or a public school in a nearby town, I decided to attend public school a few miles from the pueblo. Each day I traveled to school on a bus driven by my grandfather. Some of my friends went to BIA schools and some went to public schools. My father attended public school and my mother had gone to BIA. I was able to make my own choice as long as I took learning seriously. In my family, education was strongly stressed. I have always been surrounded by relatives who provided strong examples of what a quality education could render. My mother is a nurse, my uncle is an educator, another uncle is a surgeon, and many members of my extended family had gone on to earn college degrees.

"As the oldest, I was strongly urged to continue my education, so I embarked on a program that would include all the college preparatory classes I would need to ensure my entrance into a college or university. Even at the high school level, I enjoyed science and knew that would be my field of concentration.

"During the summer of my junior year in high school, I attended the Minority Introduction to Engineering course at New Mexico State University. I was exposed to all the different types of engineering. Civil engineering easily became my choice because I always loved the outdoors. I knew I wouldn't be happy sitting at a desk or computer all the time.

"After high school, I enrolled at New Mexico State, since I had received a positive introduction to its engineering program. In addition, my uncle worked there, I had friends going to school there, and it was my home state. Happily, I was awarded a four-year Professional Guild Scholarship from the U.S. Health Service. Thus, I became a freshman there in the fall of 1979. The scholarship paid for all my undergraduate education, but in return I was obligated to work for the agency for four years following my graduation.

"After receiving my bachelor of science degree in environmental engineering, I was assigned to the city of Tuba, Arizona, on a Navajo Indian reservation. As a field engineer, I was responsible for planning and organizing the construction of sanitation facilities and bringing in waterlines for individual families. I found it to be very rewarding work, and it seems that the Navajos agreed. When I left, they presented me with an achievement medal for the work I did during those four years.

"A typical day consists of working on the plans and designs for a pueblo spring house, spending time with the surveyors who are doing the groundwork for some of my projects, working on specifications or proposals for future projects, dealing with contractors, or helping out the other engineers when they have any technical questions.

"Another of my focuses is my membership in the Commission Corps of the Public Health Service, one of the branches of the military. We have uniforms just like the navy. Upon finishing my bachelor of science degree, I had a choice of entering as a civil service employee or applying for the Commission Corps. I elected to apply for the Commission Corps because I was told that I would probably advance more quickly that way. Today I hold the rank of lieutenant commander.

"In August of 1988, I transferred to the Pacific Northwest and worked with three different tribes, assuming the same duties as I had previously. I was the only field engineer in the office, and it was kind of scary at first but I learned to be independent. In 1991, I was selected engineer of the year for the Portland area.

"After three years, the Indian Health Service chose me to attend long-term training to get my master's degree in environmental engineering. The offer allowed me to go to school for one year and still receive my regular yearly salary. All educational expenses were absorbed by the agency. I felt that this was such a wonderful offer, I could not turn it down.

"I returned to New Mexico State for my advanced degree. The only hard part is that you must finish in one year, and the program is really a two-year program. It's pretty difficult to keep up, but if you are dedicated to accomplishing something, you will succeed. It may not be easy, but nothing that's worth accomplishing ever is. Every time you reached a goal you've set for yourself, it's time to set another. You should always do the best you can. Just meeting minimum standards is not good enough."

Albert L. de Richmond, Mechanical Engineer

Albert L. de Richmond is associate director of Health Devices Group at ECRI of Plymouth Meeting, Pennsylvania. He earned his B.S. from Penn State, his M.S. from Virginia Tech, and did postgraduate work at Drexel University in Philadelphia. Subsequently, he received his Pennsylvania professional engineer's license in 1983.

"I thought about becoming an engineer in high school," says de Richemond. "At that time, the SATs provided some guidance on what careers best suited a person, according to scores on the test. I just missed the score that pointed to medicine. Engineering was indicated for me and was supported by my outside school interests (taking things apart to find out how they worked, building things, backyard experiments, reading about science, and working in power plants and refineries).

"I chose my particular specialty after hearing about it in my freshman year. It was presented as being the foundation of most of the other engineering disciplines and as providing a broad education. It is and did. It is also mathematically oriented and offers a way of thinking about the world and how it works.

"In graduate school, I took many additional courses that enabled me to apply for medical school, but that did not work out. However, medicine still remained an area of interest. In graduate school, I started out in biomechanical engineering, but my professor became critically ill and the program was abolished. So I became a graduate teaching assistant, a position that I found to be most enjoyable.

"Subsequently, I worked for GE Re-Entry Systems Division and for two mid-size companies that make heavy processing equipment. I enjoyed this field because I was able to experiment, to get into the field where our equipment was used, to get into the factories where we built the equipment, and to solve problems with the designs.

"During my tenure at these companies, I studied for and passed the professional engineer's exam and became licensed in Pennsylvania. This was a validation for me. I felt that it showed both me and the world that I was a capable engineer.

"Following this, I hired on with a small company as a research designer. I enjoyed setting up a prototype lab and working with relatively new computer analysis programs. Then I moved to my present organization as an evaluation engineer for a special project. Completion of this led to moving within the organization to the medical device evaluation group. This position truly unites my two areas of interest—engineering and medicine. During my forty-hour work week, I now deal with clinicians and manufacturers and help them solve problems through engineering.

"My job involves talking with people (subscribers, supervisees, managers, visitors), examining things (medical devices, computer problems, situations), interpreting information (standards, published articles), reading (draft articles for our journals and periodicals, pertinent articles), writing (articles for our journal, new standards, reports), and making decisions (what to write about, how to test something, why something happened). On a typical day, I'll spend a few minutes on many topics, bouncing from one to another as the need arises due to E-mail, office visits from coworkers, meetings, telephone calls, more information, discussions, and so forth. I am always busy, even without appearing busy, because I am continually thinking about the various things I am doing or have yet to do. Sometimes the work is relaxed, but other times it can be quite tense due to the importance of the event (deposition, personnel issue). There is also the risk of catching a disease from contaminated equipment received for accident investigation.

"Our environment is casual and friendly. Most everyone has his or her own office, and none have doors. Anyone can ask anyone else for information or help at any time. We all have beepers, and the building has telephones everywhere so we can be in instant contact should a customer need our expertise. Most of us have access to the building twenty-four–seven and do come in after normal hours to do some odd jobs.

"The best aspects of my job involve the variety of work, the ability to help others and have a positive effect on something, and the people I work with—who are all very intelligent and capable.

"I would recommend that others who are interested in this field read voraciously and widely. Go to college and learn how to think. Pick a subject and study it, but don't expect to use all of it in the workaday world. Be a generalist. Learn how to multitask. Figure out how to control stress. Become flexible in thinking and in body. Learn about people and how they operate. And last but not least—learn how to balance the important things in your life."

For More Information

A number of engineering technology-related organizations provide information on engineering technician and technology careers. The agency below serves as a central distribution point for information from most of these organizations. Enclose a self-addressed, business size envelope with six first-class stamps to obtain a sampling of materials available.

The Junior Engineering Technical Society (JETS)
1420 King Street, Suite 405
Alexandria, VA 22314
http://www.asee.org/jets

Those wanting more detailed information should contact societies representing the individual branches of engineering.

American Institute of Aeronautics and Astronautics, Inc.
1801 Alexander Bell Drive, Suite 500
Reston, VA 20191

American Institute of Chemical Engineers
345 East Forty-seventh Street
New York, NY 10017

American Chemical Society
Department of Career Services
1155 Sixteenth Street NW
Washington, DC 20036

American Society of Civil Engineers
1801 Alexander Bell Drive
Reston, VA 20191

Institute of Electrical and Electronics Engineers
1828 L Street NW, Suite 1202
Washington, DC 20036

Institute of Industrial Engineers, Inc.
25 Technology Park
Norcross, GA 30092

The American Society of Mechanical Engineers
345 East Forty-seventh Street
New York, NY 10017

The Minerals, Metals, & Materials Society
420 Commonwealth Drive
Warrendale, PA 15086

ASM International (formerly American Society for Metals)
Student Outreach Program
Materials Park, OH 44073

The Society for Mining, Metallurgy, and Exploration, Inc.
P.O. Box 625002
Littleton, CO 80162

American Nuclear Society
555 North Kensington Avenue
LaGrange Park, IL 60525

Society of Petroleum Engineers
P.O. Box 833836
Richardson, TX 75083

CHAPTER EIGHT

Careers in Computer Science and Mathematics

The new electronic interdependence rewrites the world in the image of a global village. MARSHALL MCLUHAN

Help Wanted—Senior Business Systems Analyst
We are currently seeking a business systems analyst for a permanent position in the Midwest to work directly with management and users to analyze, specify, and design business applications. He or she will be in charge of developing detailed functional specifications using structured design methodologies and computer-aided system engineering tools. The successful candidate will assist the organization in establishing operational procedures and redefining work flows. He or she will frequently discuss technical and business system issues with project leaders, project teams, consultants, management, and users and is expected to provide technical direction to the more junior business systems analysts.

Qualified candidates will have a bachelor's degree in MIS, engineering, business, computer science, or a related scientific or technical discipline. Seven to ten years of experience in developing information systems is required. A master's degree in a related field will be considered equivalent to two years of experience.

Welcome to the World of Computer Science

The rapid spread of computers and computer-based technologies over the past two decades has generated a need for skilled, highly trained workers to design and develop hardware and software systems and to incorporate these advances into new or existing systems. Although many narrow specializations have developed and no uniform job titles exist, this professional specialty group is widely referred to as computer scientists and systems analysts.

Computer Scientists

Computer scientists include computer engineers, database administrators, computer support analysts, and a variety of other specialized professionals. Computer scientists are responsible for designing computers, conducting research to improve their design or use, and developing and adapting principles for applying computers to new uses. Computer scientists perform many of the same duties as other computer workers throughout a normal workday, but their jobs are distinguished by the higher level of theoretical expertise and innovation they apply to complex problems and the creation or application of new technology.

Professionals in this group who are employed by academic institutions work in areas ranging from theory to hardware to language design. Some work on multidiscipline projects, such as developing and advancing uses for virtual reality. Their counterparts in private industry work in areas such as applying theory, developing specialized languages, or designing programming tools, knowledge-based systems, or computer games.

Computer engineers work with the hardware and software aspects of systems design and development. Computer engineers may often work as part of a team that designs new computing devices or computer-related equipment.

Database administrators work with database management systems software. They reorganize and restructure data to better suit the needs of users. They also may be responsible for system security and maintaining the efficiency of the database and may aid in design implementation.

Computer support analysts provide assistance and advice to users, interpreting problems and providing technical support for hardware, software, and systems. They may work within an organization or directly for the computer or software vendor.

Systems Analysts

Systems analysts use their knowledge and skills in a problem-solving capacity, implementing the means for computer technology to meet the individual needs of an organization. They study business, scientific, or engineering data processing problems and design new solutions using computers. This process may include planning and developing new computer systems or devising ways to apply existing systems to operations now completed manually or by some less-efficient method. Systems analysts may design entirely new systems, including both hardware and software, or add a single new software application to harness more of the computer's power. They work to help an organization realize the maximum benefit from its investment in equipment, personnel, and business processes.

How Systems Analysts Work

Analysts begin an assignment by discussing the data processing problem with managers and users to determine its exact nature. A considerable amount of time is devoted to clearly defining the goals of the system and understanding the individual steps used in the process. This way the problem can be broken down into separate programmable procedures. Analysts then use various techniques, such as structured analysis, data modeling, information engineering, mathematical model building, sampling, and cost accounting. It is important to specify the files and records to be accessed by the system and design the processing steps as well as the format for the output that will meet the users' needs. Once the design has been developed, systems analysts prepare charts and diagrams that describe it in terms that managers and other users can understand. They may prepare cost-benefit and return-on-investment analyses to help management decide whether the proposed system will be satisfactory as well as financially feasible.

When a system is accepted, systems analysts may determine what computer hardware and software will be needed to set up the system or implement changes to it. They coordinate tests and observe initial use of the system to ensure that it performs as planned. They prepare specifications, work diagrams, and structure charts for computer programmers to follow and then work with them to "debug," or eliminate errors from, the system.

Some organizations do not employ programmers; instead, a single worker called a programmer-analyst is responsible for both systems analysis and programming. As this becomes more commonplace, analysts will increasingly work with computer-aided software engineering (CASE) tools, object-oriented programming languages, and client-server applications, as well as multimedia and Internet technology.

One obstacle associated with expanding computer use is the inability of different computers to communicate with one other. Many systems analysts are involved with connecting all the computers in an individual office, department, or establishment. This "networking" has many variations and may be referred to as local area networks, wide area networks, or multiuser systems. A primary goal of networking is to allow users of microcomputers, also known as personal computers or PCs, to retrieve data from a mainframe computer and use it on their machines. This connection also allows data to be entered into the mainframe from the PC and accessed by other users on the network.

Because up-to-date information—accounting records, sales figures, or budget projections, for example—is so important in modern organizations, systems analysts may be instructed to make the computer systems in each department compatible so that facts and figures can be shared. Similarly, electronic mail requires open pathways to send messages, documents, and data from one computer "mailbox" to another across different equipment and program lines. Analysts must design the gates in hardware and software to allow free exchange of data and custom applications as well as the computer power to process it all. They study the seemingly incompatible pieces and create ways to link them so users can access information from any part of the system.

Mathematicians

Mathematicians are a part of one of the oldest and most basic of the sciences. They are charged with the responsibility of creating new mathematical theories and techniques involving the latest technology and solving economic, scientific, engineering, and business problems using mathematical knowledge and computational tools.

Mathematical work falls into two broad classes: theoretical (pure) mathematics and applied mathematics. However, these classes are not sharply defined and often overlap.

Theoretical mathematicians advance mathematical science by developing new principles and new relationships between existing principles of mathematics. Although they seek to increase basic knowledge without necessarily considering its practical use, this pure and abstract knowledge has been instrumental in producing or furthering many scientific and engineering achievements.

Applied mathematicians use theories and techniques, such as mathematical modeling and computational methods, to formulate and solve practical problems in business, government, engineering, and the physical, life, and social sciences. For example, they may analyze the mathematical aspects of computer and communications networks, the effects of new drugs on disease, the aerodynamic characteristics of aircraft, or the distribution costs or manufacturing processes of businesses. When confronted with difficult problems, applied mathematicians working in industrial research and development may develop or enhance mathematical methods. Some mathematicians, called cryptanalysts, analyze and decipher encryption systems designed to transmit national security-related information.

Mathematicians use computers extensively to analyze relationships among variables, solve complex problems, develop models, and process large amounts of data.

Much work in applied mathematics is carried on by persons other than mathematicians. In fact, because mathematics is the foundation upon which many other academic disciplines are built, the number of workers using mathematical techniques is many times greater than the number actually designated as mathematicians. Engineers, computer scientists, physicists, and economists are among those who use mathematics extensively but have job titles other than mathematician. Some workers, such as statisticians, actuaries, and operations research analysts, actually are specialists in a particular branch of mathematics.

Education and Training

Computer Scientists and Systems Analysts

There is no universally accepted way to prepare for a job as a computer professional because employers' preferences depend on the work to be done. Many people develop advanced computer skills in other occupations in which they work extensively with computers and then transfer into computer occupations. For example, an accountant may become a systems analyst specializing in accounting systems development, or an individual may move into a systems analyst job after working as computer programmer.

Employers almost always seek college graduates for computer professional positions; for some of the more complex jobs, persons with graduate degrees are preferred. Generally, a doctorate, or at least a master's degree, in computer science or engineering is required for computer scientist jobs in research laboratories or academic institutions. Some computer scientists are able to gain sufficient experience for this type of position with only a bachelor's degree, but this is difficult. Computer engineers generally require a bachelor's degree in computer engineering, electrical engineering, or math. Computer support analysts may also need a bachelor's degree in a computer-related field, as well as significant experience working with computers, including programming skills.

For systems analyst or even database administrator positions, many employers seek applicants who have a bachelor's degree in computer science, information science, computer information systems, or data processing. Regardless of college major, employers generally look for people who are familiar with programming languages and have broad knowledge of and experience with computer systems and technologies. Courses in computer programming or systems design offer good preparation for a job in this field. For jobs in a business environment, employers usually want systems analysts to have a background in business management or a closely related field, while a background in the physical sciences, applied mathematics, or engineering is preferred for work in scientifically oriented organizations.

Systems analysts must be able to concentrate, think logically, have good communication skills, and like working with ideas and people. Since they must often deal with a number of tasks simultaneously, they need to be organized and detail minded. Although both computer scientists and systems analysts often work independently, they also may work in teams on large projects. Thus, they must be able to communicate effectively with computer personnel, such as programmers and managers, as well as with other staff who have little or no technical computer background.

Technological advances come so rapidly in the computer field that continuous study is necessary to keep skills up to date. Continuing education is usually offered by employers, hardware and software vendors, colleges and universities, or private training institutions. Additional training may come from professional development seminars offered by professional computing societies.

The Institute for Certification of Computing Professionals offers the designation Certified Computing Professional (CCP) to those who have at least four years of work experience as a computer professional or at least two years of experience and a college degree. Candidates must pass a core examination that tests general knowledge plus exams in two specialty areas (or in one specialty area and two computer programming languages). The Quality Assurance Institute awards the designation Certified Quality Analyst (CQA) to those who meet education and experience requirements, pass an exam, and endorse a code of ethics. Neither designation is mandatory, but professional certification may provide a job seeker a competitive advantage.

Computer engineers and scientists employed in industry may eventually advance into managerial or project leadership positions. Those employed in academic institutions can become heads of research departments or published authorities in their fields. Computer professionals with several years of experience and considerable expertise in a particular area may choose to start their own computer consulting firms.

After several years of service, systems analysts may be promoted to senior or lead systems analysts. Those who show leadership ability also can advance to management positions such as manager of information systems or chief information officer.

Mathematicians

A bachelor's degree in mathematics is the minimum education needed for prospective mathematicians. In the federal government, entry-level job candidates usually need to have a four-year degree with a major in mathematics or a four-year degree with the equivalent of a mathematics major (twenty-four semester hours of mathematics courses).

In private industry, job candidates generally need a master's or a doctoral degree to obtain jobs as mathematicians. Most positions designated for mathematicians are in research and development labs as part of technical teams. These research scientists engage in either pure mathematical (basic) research or in applied research focusing on developing or improving specific products or processes. The majority of bachelor's and master's degree holders in private industry work not as mathematicians but in related fields, such as computer science, where they are called computer programmers, systems analysts, or systems engineers.

A bachelor's degree in mathematics is offered by most colleges and universities. Mathematics courses usually required for this degree are calculus, differential equations, and linear and abstract algebra. Additional course work might include probability theory and statistics, mathematical analysis, numerical analysis, topology, modern algebra, discrete mathematics, and mathematical logic. Many colleges and universities urge or even require students majoring in mathematics to take several courses in a field that uses or is closely related to mathematics, such as computer science, engineering, operations research, physical science, statistics, or economics. A double major in mathematics and another discipline, such as computer science, economics, or one of the sciences, is particularly desirable.

In graduate school, students conduct research and take advanced courses, usually specializing in a subfield of mathematics. Some areas of concentration are algebra, number theory, real or complex analysis, geometry, topology, logic, and applied mathematics.

For those in the area of applied mathematics, training in the field in which the mathematics will be used is very important. Fields that use mathematics extensively include physics, actuarial science, engineering, and operations research. Of increasing importance are computer and information science, business and industrial management, economics, statistics, chemistry, geology, life sciences, and the behavioral sciences.

Mathematicians should have substantial knowledge of computer programming because most complex mathematical computation and much mathematical modeling is done by computer. Mathematicians need good reasoning ability and persistence in order to identify, analyze, and apply basic principles to technical problems. Communication skills are also important as mathematicians must be able to interact with others, including nonmathematicians, and discuss proposed solutions to problems.

Employment Outlook

Computer Scientists and Systems Analysts

Computer scientists and systems analysts are expected to be among the fastest-growing occupations through the year 2006. Employment of computing professionals is expected to increase much faster than average as technology becomes more sophisticated and organizations continue to adopt and integrate these technologies, making for plentiful job openings. In addition, tens of thousands of job openings will result annually from the need to replace workers who move into managerial positions or other occupations or who leave the labor force.

Competition will place organizations under growing pressure to use technological advances in areas such as office and factory automation, telecommunications technology, and scientific research. As the complexity of these applications grows, more computer scientists and systems analysts will be needed to design, develop, and implement the new technology.

As more computing power is made available to the individual user, more computer scientists and systems analysts will be required to provide support. As users develop more sophisticated knowledge of computers, they become more aware of the machines' potential and better able to suggest how computers could be used to increase their own productivity and that of the organization. Increasingly, users are able to design and implement more of their own applications and programs. As technology continues to advance, computer scientists and systems analysts will continue to need to upgrade their levels of skill and technical expertise and their ability to interact with users will increase in importance.

A greater emphasis on problem solving, analysis, and client-server environments will also contribute to the growing demand for systems analysts.

Mathematicians

Employment of mathematicians is expected to increase more slowly than the average for all occupations through the year 2006. The number of jobs available for workers whose educational background is solely mathematics is not expected to increase significantly. Many firms, particularly those engaged in civilian research and development, are not planning to expand their research departments much and, in some cases, may reduce them. Anticipated reductions in defense-related research and development will also affect employment, especially in the federal government.

Those whose educational backgrounds include the study of a related discipline will have better job opportunities. However, as advancements in technology lead to expanding applications of mathematics, more workers with knowledge of mathematics will be required. Many of these workers have job titles that reflect the end product of their work rather than the discipline of mathematics used in that work.

Bachelor's degree holders in mathematics are usually not qualified for most jobs as mathematicians. If they meet state certification requirements, they may become high school mathematics teachers. Those with strong backgrounds in computer science, electrical or mechanical engineering, or operations research should have good opportunities in industry.

Those with master's degrees in mathematics will face very strong competition for jobs in theoretical research. However, job opportunities in applied mathematics and related areas such as computer programming, operations research, and engineering design in industry and government will be more numerous.

Earnings

The most recent findings from the U.S. Bureau of Labor Statistics show $50,300 as an average yearly income for computer scientists. The figure for systems analysts is $54,110 and $41,840 for mathematicians.

Parade of Professionals

Krista Jacobsen, Senior Systems Engineer

Krista Jacobsen is senior systems engineer at Amati Communications Corporation in San Jose, California. She received her bachelor of science degree in electrical engineering from the University of Denver and both her master of science and doctorate from Stanford University.

"I was attracted to electrical engineering because I found those courses to be the most challenging I had ever encountered," explains Jacobsen. "I worked harder than I ever had in school, and the extra effort really paid off—not only did I graduate with all As in major courses, but I was awarded scholarships to an outstanding graduate school and also awarded graduate fellowships.

"While working on my doctorate, I was employed at Amati as a consultant. When the time came to start interviewing for a post-graduation job, Amati was quick to make me an offer. I still interviewed at other companies but knew in advance that I wanted to stay here because the company had been very good to me. I felt a loyalty to stay and become part of its team.

"My job is somewhat unusual and hence, difficult to describe," she says. "The company considers me quite versatile for a Ph.D., and my employer knows that I enjoy doing many difficult things, including tasks not traditionally associated with electrical engineers, such as writing and public speaking and working on heavy technical problems. My particular responsibilities include designing and managing the company's website; writing and running computer simulations to project the performance of our systems; investigating alternative solutions and creating new products; attending standards meetings (for which I write and present technical contributions); and offering technical support as necessary to the sales and marketing departments, which frequently requires travel to other companies or to conferences. On the road once or twice a month, I give presentations and/or attend meetings. At the office, I spend a lot of time writing, as ideas are useless unless they can be communicated to others. I often write internal documents explaining the problems I've been looking at and the solutions that I and my colleagues prepare.

"My advice is to work hard so you can reap the rewards. Many people drop out of engineering programs because some of the courses seem so difficult. The key is to survive the nasty courses and excel in the courses you enjoy. The road gets easier and more interesting as you progress, and eventually you'll find out that a career in engineering is fun, rewarding, and challenging."

Carol Prochnow, Senior Section Manager

Carol Prochnow is senior section manager at Schlumberger Well Services. She received her bachelor of science degree in electrical and computer engineering from the University of Michigan in Ann Arbor and her master of science degree in computer science from Cornell in Ithaca, New York.

"When I was going to middle and high school, the computing profession was still in its infancy. My older brother was taking a class in FORTRAN programming language, and I happened to look at the book and became fascinated by the whole idea of programming. I'd always loved math but didn't see a career there. Computer science, however, seemed very attractive and looked like a career that would be viable for many years.

"I am an engineering manager for about twenty people," she says. "We are responsible for the data acquisition and analysis software for a service industry called 'oil well logging,' Schlumberger's core business. When an oil company drills a well, it isn't like in movies, when a huge gusher begins to spew oil into the sky. In fact, they sometimes do not know if there are hydrocarbons or where they are. Schlumberger is hired to perform a service where advanced sensors are lowered into the oil well bore, connected via a conducting cable to a computer system on the surface. My section is responsible for the 'middleware' software that sits on top of this computer's operating system. This software provides data acquisition, data management, task control, and graphics facilities to support different sensors. It is loaded into the computer system either in a truck or an offshore unit.

"A typical day is split between responding to E-mail, attending technical meetings, reviewing documents, Web surfing, programming and debugging, and talking on the phone. Since I love to build things, I'm really glad that this is also an integral part of my job. We take our projects all the way from requirements analysis through delivery to our field organization.

"I would advise interested candidates to get good grades. Grades are what you need to get your foot in the door of a good job. Schlumberger does not even look at resumes that have less than a B+ average.

"Continuing your education is always a plus. And internships are very valuable. In my own case, I feel that my master's degree helped me to get this job and also provided me with some skills I didn't have when I finished my undergraduate program.

"It's a good idea to work at a variety of companies during summer breaks. You'll learn a lot and also find out if you like working with the same individuals day after day. If not, engineering is probably not for you."

Steven Brent Assa, Research Scientist

Steven Assa is a research scientist. He earned his bachelor of arts degree in mathematics and Scandinavian literature and his doctorate in mathematics from Ohio State University in Columbus.

"I have known since I was a child that I would be a scientist. When I was very small, I thought that meant that I would be a medical doctor (psychiatrist, to be exact). I held that belief until I got to college and discovered that what I really liked was mathematics and Scandinavian literature (Ibsen and Strindberg). Mathematics appealed to me because I thought that God spoke to people through universal laws that were conveyed in goodness and love, through mathematical equations. Understanding these equations was the same as understanding the way the world is, which is a first step to accepting the beings in the world.

"My current job is the most wonderful job that I can imagine," he says. "I may sound over the top on this, but over the past five years I have begun to see the beauty of mathematics in the physics applications that I work on at a level that makes me honored to think that I understand even a small part of their beauty and organic purpose.

"I spend about eight hours at my office, but I spend many more hours a day thinking about the meaning and elegance of the equations that I manipulate. My current project is to build a 3-D geometry modeling system for geological applications. I work with geologists, physicists, computer scientists, and other mathematicians. There are never enough hours in the day for me to talk to all the people with whom I interact.

"My typical day begins with answering mail and checking in with a junior colleague with whom I am working very closely. If he or I have questions regarding the previous day's collaboration, we review them. Otherwise, we decide what aspect of the project to consider, decide who looks at which issues, then separate for a few hours. I make notes, decide how to approach my projects, and then close my door and get immersed. Interruptions break my concentration, but part of the fun of this job is receiving new issues from users of the computer system that I have built.

"The work is very pleasant, but I do get mentally drained from the heavy mental exertion of this work. When this happens, I pull down one of my 'classical' mathematical physics books to gain a sense of clarity and to give myself a chance to avoid my immediate problems for a few minutes.

"In a sentence, I have a job that permits me to be a permanent graduate student research assistant, with myself as the boss. Most of all I like the idea that I am able to propose the majority of my work. However, my work is not open-ended—far from it. I work on projects that have a very visible payoff for my company, but I am able to focus on the parts that are exciting to me. I am trusted and have the respect of my management. I have no managerial urge, and the company has not tried to force me into this level.

"The least agreeable part of what I do is to make certain that I am not drafted back into the day-to-day engineering ranks of the company. I did that for about nine years, and it was certainly good training in general computer systems design, product completion, and group effort, but today I need time to dream. Fortunately, after my first patent was issued, the company realized that my talents could be used more efficiently in my present position.

"I would recommend that you never lose your need to understand why things are the way they are. Talk to people about your ideas and spend your time trying to make something useful out of them. Read, read, read—especially the classics. Clarity of thought is timeless and independent of the problem addressed."

For More Information

Further information about computer careers is available from:

Association for Computing Machinery
1515 Broadway
New York, NY 10036

Information about the designation Certified Computing Professional is available from:

Institute for the Certification of Computing Professionals
2200 East Devon Avenue, Suite 268
Des Plaines, IL 60018

Information about the designation Certified Quality Analyst is available from:

Quality Assurance Institute
7575 Phillips Boulevard, Suite 350
Orlando, FL 32819

For additional information about mathematics career opportunities and professional training, contact:

American Mathematical Society
Department of Professional Programs and Services
P.O. Box 6248
Providence, RI 02940

Conference Board of the Mathematical Sciences
1529 Eighteenth Street NW
Washington, DC 20036
(Ask for the resource guide on careers in the mathematical
sciences.)

Mathematical Association of America
1529 Eighteenth Street NW
Washington, DC 20036

Society for Industrial and Applied Mathematics
3600 University City Science Center
Philadelphia, PA 19104

CHAPTER NINE

Careers in Music

When I hear music, I fear no danger. I am invulnerable. I see no foe. I am related to the earliest times, and to the latest.
HENRY DAVID THOREAU

Help Wanted—Musician

Our local orchestra is seeking a talented, experienced musician who can play the piano with skill and a desire to "touch" those who are listening. Only those who qualify should contact us.

Ah—the power of music. It moves us to weep and to feel inspired. It stirs up memories of days past and precious moments of joy and sadness. Truly, those who can move us to these levels are gifted geniuses.

Welcome to the World of Musicians

Musicians may play musical instruments, sing, compose, arrange, or conduct groups in instrumental or vocal performances. They may perform alone or as part of a group, before live audiences or on radio, or in recording studios, television, or movie productions.

Musicians may specialize in a particular kind of music or performance. Instrumental musicians play a musical instrument in an orchestra, band, rock group, or jazz group. Classical musicians may perform with professional orchestras or in small chamber music groups like quartets or trios. Musicians may play any of a wide variety of string, brass, woodwind, or percussion instruments or electronic synthesizers. These talented professionals may learn how to play several related instruments, such as flute and clarinet, thus improving their employment opportunities.

Singers interpret music using their knowledge of voice production, melody, and harmony. They may sing character parts or perform in their own individual styles. Often classified according to their voice range—soprano, contralto, tenor, baritone, or bass—singers may also be classified by the type of music they sing, such as opera, rock and roll, reggae, folk, rap, or country and western.

Orchestra conductors lead instrumental music groups, such as orchestras, dance bands, and various popular ensembles. Conductors audition and select musicians, choose the music to accommodate the talents and abilities of the musicians, and direct rehearsals and performances, applying conducting techniques to achieve desired musical effects.

Musicians often perform at night and on weekends and spend considerable time in practice and rehearsal. Performances frequently require travel. Because many musicians find only part-time work or experience unemployment between engagements, they often supplement their income with other types of jobs. In fact, many decide they cannot support themselves as musicians and take permanent, full-time jobs in other occupations while working only part-time as musicians.

Nearly three out of five musicians who are employed work part-time; more than one out of four are self-employed. Many work in cities in which entertainment and recording activities are concentrated, such as New York, Los Angeles, and Nashville. Musicians may work in opera, musical comedy, and ballet productions. Many are organists who play in churches or synagogues. Two out of three musicians who are paid a salary work in religious organizations.

Musicians also perform in clubs and restaurants and for weddings and other events. Well-known musicians and groups give their own concerts, appear live on radio and television, make recordings and music videos, or go on concert tours. The armed forces, too, offer careers in their bands and smaller musical groups.

Education and Training

Many people who become professional musicians begin studying an instrument at an early age. They may gain valuable experience playing in a school or community band or orchestra or with a group of friends.

Singers usually start training when their voices mature. Participation in school musicals or in choirs often provides good early training and experience.

Musicians need extensive and prolonged training to acquire the necessary skill, knowledge, and ability to interpret music. This training may be obtained through private study with an accomplished musician, in a college or university music program, in a music conservatory, or through practice with a group. For study in an institution, an audition frequently is necessary. Formal courses include musical theory, music interpretation, composition, conducting, and instrumental and voice instruction.

Many colleges, universities, and music conservatories grant bachelor's or higher degrees in music. Many also grant degrees in music education to qualified graduates who then obtain a state certificate to teach music in an elementary or secondary school.

Young people who are considering careers in music should have musical talent, versatility, creative ability, poise, and the stage presence to face large audiences.

Since quality performance requires constant study and practice, self-discipline is vital. Moreover, musicians who play concert and nightclub engagements must have physical stamina because frequent travel and night performances are required. They must also be prepared to face the anxiety of intermittent employment and rejections when auditioning for work.

Advancement for musicians generally means becoming better known and performing for greater earnings with better-known bands and orchestras. Successful musicians often rely on agents or managers to find them performing engagements, negotiate contracts, and plan their careers.

Employment Outlook

Competition for musician jobs is keen, and talent alone is no guarantee of success. The glamour and potentially high earnings in this occupation attract many talented individuals. However, being able to play several instruments and types of music enhances a musician's employment prospects.

Overall, employment of musicians is expected to grow faster than the average for all occupations through the year 2006. Almost all new wage and salary jobs for musicians will arise in religious organizations and bands, orchestras, and other entertainment groups. A decline in employment is projected for salaried musicians in restaurants and bars, although they comprise a very small proportion of all salaried musicians. Bars, which regularly employ musicians, are expected to grow more slowly than eating establishments because consumption of alcoholic beverages outside the home is expected to continue to decline. Overall, most job openings for musicians will arise from the need to replace those who leave the field each year because they are unable to make a living solely as musicians.

Earnings

Earnings often depend on a performer's professional reputation, place of employment, and on the number of hours worked. The most successful musicians can earn far more than the minimum salaries indicated below.

According to the American Federation of Musicians, minimum salaries in major orchestras ranges from about $22,000 to $90,000 per year. Each orchestra works out a separate contract with its local union. Top orchestras have sessions that range from twenty-nine to fifty-two weeks, or a full year, with most major orchestras working fifty-two weeks. In regional orchestras, minimum salaries are between $8,000 and $22,000 per year; the season lasts seven to forty-eight weeks, with an average of thirty-five weeks. In contrast, community orchestras have more limited levels of funding and thus offer salaries that are much lower and for shorter seasons.

Musicians employed by some symphony orchestras work under master wage agreements, which guarantee a season's work up to fifty-two weeks. Many other musicians may face relatively long periods of unemployment between jobs.

Even when employed, however, many work part-time. Thus, their earnings generally are lower than those in many other occupations. Moreover, since they may not work steadily for one employer, some performers cannot qualify for unemployment compensation, and few have either sick leave or vacations with pay. For these reasons, many musicians give private lessons or take jobs unrelated to music to supplement their earnings as performers.

Many musicians belong to a local of the American Federation of Musicians. Professional singers usually belong to a branch of the Associated Actors and Artists of America.

Parade of Professionals

Ed Goeke, Music Director

Ed Goeke is the music director of Christ Episcopal Church in Overland Park, Kansas. He has both a B.A. and an M.A. in music education from the University of Iowa, and an M.A. from the University of Kansas in Lawrence, where he is a Ph.D. candidate in music education.

"I studied voice, piano, and French horn from the time I was in junior high school," says Goeke. "Both of my parents are music educators, so it was a natural thing for me to enter a career in music. Music has affected my whole life. It is my life. I can't imagine not having musical outlets. I will probably never leave music. What I find most gratifying is performing well, knowing that people are grateful for a job well done.

"Sunday is the culmination of the work I do all week. The day starts around 8:00 A.M. with warm-up for the first service at 8:45 A.M. This is an ensemble of eight to ten people. When this service is over, then rehearsal starts (9:30 or so) for the 10:45 service. This is a choir of twenty-four people with an organist. The service is over around noon. There is a break for lunch, then around 2:30 rehearsal starts for the 5:30 service. We organize and plan for this week's service and some for next week's selection. The day usually ends around 7:00 P.M.

"It's very casual here in terms of dress and chain of command. A great deal of time is spent in rehearsal and planning for worship services. The busiest time is the whole month of December due to the number of liturgies and the importance of the spiritual services.

"I took this job because it enables me to use my classical background and work in a traditional setting but at the same time lead others in contemporary music. It's great working with this fine group of people who offer a variety of musical talent. I like working with a mission in mind—having a goal of bringing people closer to God through worship by providing windows of opportunity through excellent music. What I like least is reproducing music and having to stay on top of all of the paperwork.

"Church jobs are changing dramatically. The best way to be equipped is to get very good at one thing. If you want to be a music director of a church full-time, then it is important to have excellent keyboarding skills. I'd recommend gaining skills in arranging and improvisational skills and exposure to a wide variety of music. It is important to be able to work well with people. This can be accomplished by performing in church choirs and acquiring experience.

"It's important that you are a people person, that you are a team builder and a consensus builder, that you are sensitive to people's needs, that you have a thorough knowledge of what makes music good, and that you have a background in performance. Also desirable is a solid knowledge of literature for choirs, a background in liturgy, the ability to take available resources and arrange on the spot, the ability to communicate effectively, and good organizations skills."

Priscilla Gale, Opera Singer

Soprano Priscilla Gale attended both the Juilliard School of Music and the Cleveland Institute of Music. She has also studied in Austria and with private teachers Luigi Ricci (in Rome) and Michael Trimble. Currently, when she's not performing with an opera company or symphony orchestra, she is a faculty member at Wesleyan University in Middletown, Connecticut, where she teaches voice.

"Having come from a very musical family of pianists, singers, and violinists, I was at the piano at the age of five. My family always assumed that I would pursue a career as a pianist, but I realized my real joy and fulfillment was in singing, not at the

piano. As I began to explore that world more thoroughly, I discovered opera, and I found my home. The rest is history. I
received my first professional contract with the Ft. Wayne (Indiana) Symphony Orchestra during my senior year at Cleveland
Institute of Music.

"Every engagement a singer or performer receives changes you
in the most wonderful way. You, as an artist, grow on multiple
levels—personally, inwardly and artistically, outwardly—and one
thing leads to another. Each time, your life as an artist is
changed; you grow in some immeasurable, wonderful way, and
the possibilities are limitless.

"No one job site is like another. In opera, the rehearsals are
intense, with the appropriate union breaks, but with long, long
days, usually exceeding ten to twelve hours over a period of two
weeks or three weeks. It really depends on how a company works,
and they all work differently.

"Orchestra jobs tend to be over a three- or four-day period.
Usually you have a piano rehearsal with the conductor, then
there are one or two orchestra rehearsals, followed by the performances. It is always busy and intense, but exciting. It is fast
paced, and one must know one's craft. There is little room for
poor preparation. And you must always have the ability to adjust
to every circumstance and environment, for no two are ever the
same. Every conductor is different, every director, and so forth.
You must be very adaptable and professional.

"What I love most about my work is the ability to touch an
audience—people I never meet individually, but collectively. My
heart and soul meets theirs. But there are just not enough performance opportunities for everyone, and it is no longer possible
to make a full-time living at this career, unless you are one of the
lucky top 20 percent.

"I always tell people who want to do this kind of work to look
inward and ask if there is anything else in life that will bring
them happiness and fulfillment. If so, then I suggest that they do
that instead. If not, then they should by all means pursue this

career. But know that it is—especially in the beginning—a very difficult business and a difficult life.

"Talent is but a small piece of it. Most people cannot comprehend the level of sacrifice that this career requires. There is that wonderful, romantic notion of being the 'starving artist,' but there's nothing romantic about it when you're living it.

"With hard work, determination, perseverance, and an unwavering faith in yourself, anything can happen. The journey is an incredible ride and one I would not have missed. And as I look back at my past, at my present, and toward my future, I can honestly say that I am one of the lucky ones."

For More Information

There are literally hundreds of professional associations for musicians. Contact any of the following for more information about employment in this field.

American Federation of Musicians (AFM)
1501 Broadway, Suite 600
New York, NY 10036

American Federation of Television and Radio Artists (AFTRA)
260 Madison Avenue
New York, NY 10016

American Guild of Musical Artists (AGMA)
1727 Broadway
New York, NY 10019

American Guild of Organists (AGO)
475 Riverside Drive, Suite 1260
New York, NY 10115

American Guild of Music (AGM)
5354 Washington Street, Box 3
Downers Grove, IL 60515

American Music Conference (AMC)
5140 Avenida Encinas
Carlsbad, CA 92008

American Musicological Society
201 South Thirty-fourth Street
University of Pennsylvania
Philadelphia, PA 19104

American Symphony Orchestra League (ASOL)
777 Fourteenth Street NW, Suite 500
Washington, DC 20005

Association of Canadian Orchestras
56 The Esplanade, Suite 311
Toronto, Canada M5E IA7

Black Music Association (BMA)
1775 Broadway
New York, NY 10019

Broadcast Music, Inc. (BMI)
320 West Fifty-seventh Street
New York, NY 10019

Chamber Music America
545 Eighth Avenue
New York, NY 10018

Chorus America
Association of Professional Vocal Ensembles
2111 Sansom Street
Philadelphia, PA 19103

College Music Society
202 West Spruce
Missoula, MT 59802

Concert Artists Guild (CAG)
850 Seventh Avenue, Room 1003
New York, NY 10019

International Conference of Symphony and Opera
    Musicians (ICSOM)
6607 Waterman
St. Louis, MO 63130

Metropolitan Opera Association (MOA)
Lincoln Center
New York, NY 10023

National Academy of Popular Music (NAPM)
885 Second Avenue
New York, NY 10017

National Academy of Recording Arts and Sciences (NARAS)
303 North Glen Oaks Boulevard, Suite 140
Burbank, CA 91502

National Association of Music Theaters
John F. Kennedy Center for the Performing Arts
Washington, DC 20566

National Association of Schools of Music
11250 Roger Bacon Drive, Suite 21
Reston, VA 22091

National Orchestral Association (NOA)
474 Riverside Drive, Room 455
New York, NY 10115

National Symphony Orchestra Association (NSOA)
John F. Kennedy Center for the Performing Arts
Washington, DC 20566

Opera America
777 Fourteenth Street NW, Suite 520
Washington, DC 20005

Society of Professional Audio Recording Studios
4300 Tenth Avenue North, #2
Lake Worth, FL 33461

Screen Actors Guild (SAG)
7065 Hollywood Boulevard
Hollywood, CA 90028

Touring Entertainment Industry Association (TEIA)
1203 Lake Street
Fort Worth, TX 76102

Women in Music
P.O. Box 441
Radio City Station
New York, NY 10101

CHAPTER TEN

Careers in Art

An artist is a dreamer consenting to dream of the actual world.
GEORGE SANTAYANA

Help Wanted—Artists
Artists wanted to paint wall murals in children's bedrooms.
Experience required. Reply to Box 643 at this newspaper.

T he genius of history's greatest artists—Leonardo da
Vinci, Michelangelo, Rembrandt, and scores of others—
has left us with a legacy of indescribable beauty and
deeper questions and insights into both the plight and th ejoys of
human existence. Perhaps the true genious of art is its universal
appeal to people all over the world. Even today's artists face the
test of time and, to a great degree, use their genius to challenge
our perceptions of society, culture, human relationships—even
the essence of art itself.

Welcome to the World of Art

Your love of color, along with your artistic talent and skill, has
led you toward a career as a practicing artist. Your goal is to be
able to create works of art that allow for self-expression and the
need to make a living. Perhaps you even long to open your own
studio, a place in which to create and sell your work. Whether
it's pottery or painting, sewing or stained glass, artists and artisans can make a name for themselves and work full-time in their

chosen areas—without necessarily starving in the proverbial artist's garret.

Having said that, few studio artists can move immediately into a career that provides adequate financial support, at least not at first. It takes time to build a reputation or a clientele and during those "lean years," many artists seek out additional employment so they can be assured of a regular paycheck.

But whether you're moonlighting in other areas or are able to devote yourself fully to your art, you probably have questions about the different forms of studio art and the options for employment.

Studio Artists

Painters

Painters generally work on canvas, producing two-dimensional art forms, though they are not restricted to this alone. Some perform their painting on furniture or clothing. Others specialize in wall murals. In the end, painters' surfaces are limited only by their imaginations.

Painters study and use the techniques of shading, perspective, and color mixing. They may produce works that portray realistic scenes, or they may choose to work with more abstract depictions, evoking different moods and emotions. The materials they use include oils, watercolors, acrylics, pastels, magic markers, pencils, pen and ink, charcoal, and pastels.

Sculptors

Sculptors work with three-dimensional art forms, either molding and joining materials such as clay, glass, wire, plastic, or metal or cutting and carving forms from a block of plaster, wood, stone, and even ice. Some sculptors combine materials such as concrete, metal, wood, plastic, and paper.

Potters

Potters work with a variety of clays—from low-fire clays to high-fire stoneware or porcelain—and either hand build their artwork or create different forms using a potter's wheel. Those using the wheel have the choice of electric wheels or kickwheels. They may work in production, turning out large numbers of the same item, or they may create only one-of-a-kind pieces. The process includes drying and trimming the pieces, firing them, then glazing them for a final firing. Potters may follow existing glaze recipes or experiment with different chemicals to formulate their own.

Printmakers

Printmakers create printed images on fabric, paper, or other media. They use designs cut into wood, stone, or metal or from computer-driven data. The designs may be engraved (as in the case of woodblocking); etched (as in the production of etchings); or derived from computers in the form of inkjet or laser prints.

Stained-Glass Artists

Stained-glass artists work with glass, paints, leading, wood, and other materials to create functional as well as decorative artwork such as windows, skylights, or doors. They repair existing stained- glass windows or produce new designs.

Photographers

Photographers use a variety of equipment when taking photographs, including cameras, lenses, film, filters, tripods, flash guns, and light meters. Those who perform their own darkroom work use chemicals and paper in much the same way a painter uses paint and canvas. They capture realistic scenes of people, places, and events, or through the use of various techniques, both natural and contrived, they can also create special effects.

Woodworkers

Woodworkers create furniture or accessories such as jewelry boxes, bowls, and picture frames. The saying goes that a woodworker is only as good as his or her tools. Some choose to work with only hand tools, such as planers and chisels. Others stock their workshops with a full array of power tools, including table saws, joiners, and sanders. They also use a variety of oils, paints, stains, and varnishes.

Other Crafts

There is a myriad of other art and craft forms, including weaving, needlepoint, crewel, quilting, rugmaking, basketweaving, papier-mâché, tole, and dollmaking. Artisans work with a variety of materials in producing their art.

Where Can Artists Find Work?

Studios and Storefronts

Studio artists usually work independently, choosing whatever subject matter and medium suits them. Artists generally work in art and design studios located in commercial spaces or in their own home studios.

Some artists prefer to work alone; others require the stimulation of other artists working nearby. For those, sharing space with other artists is often a viable alternative to the lone studio—

both for stimulation and for economic reasons, since shared space will cost the artist less money. There is a trend in many large cities and even in more out-of-the-way areas for artists to share space in cooperatively owned studios or in rented warehouses or storefronts that have been converted for their specific needs.

Artists with their own or shared space often have storefronts in which to sell their work. They may also depend on stores, museums, corporate collections, art galleries, and private homes as outlets for their work. Some work may be done on request from clients; others are done "on spec," with the artist making their pieces first in the hope of finding interested buyers.

Art Fairs

Some artists follow the art fair or craft fair circuit and pack up their work and tour the country on a regular basis, deriving most, if not all, of their income from this source alone. However, many artists will tell you that this option can be risky, with no guarantee of sales. In addition, the fair circuit is vulnerable to the changes in weather and the whims of impulse buyers or true art lovers and collectors.

Mail Order

There are publications that cater to almost every craft, from doll collecting to antique quilt restoration. Many artisans are familiar with these magazines that are geared toward their craft. There they can find a home to advertise their products to a targeted audience of collectors.

Living History Museums

Most living history museums employ skilled artisans—potters, silversmiths, candlemakers, wigmakers, needleworkers, costumers, woodworkers, blacksmiths, to name just a few—to demonstrate early crafts and trades. Some of these artisans perform their art while playing the role of a particular character of the time. Others wear twentieth-century clothing and discuss their craft from a modern perspective.

In addition to demonstrations, artisans often produce many of the items on display in the various exhibits or placed for sale in the museum gift shops. This includes the furniture, cookware, and sometimes even the actual buildings. Colonial Williamsburg and Plimoth Plantation are just two examples of living history museums.

Education and Training

In the fine arts field, your talent speaks for you, and there are no real formal training requirements. Those who are gifted will undoubtedly find an avenue. However, it is very difficult to become skilled enough to make a living without some basic training. Bachelor's and graduate degree programs in fine arts are offered in many colleges and universities.

In addition to the skills learned or honed, those studying in colleges or art schools make important contacts during their formal training years. Instructors are often working artists with hands-on experience and advice to offer.

Employment Outlook

The fine arts field has a glamorous and exciting image. Many people with creative ability pursue a livelihood in the various sectors of this field. As a result, there is always keen competition for both salaried and freelance work, especially in the fine arts. However, employment of fine artists is expected to grow because of population growth, rising incomes, and growth in the number of people who appreciate fine arts. Graphic arts studios, clients, and galleries alike are always on the lookout for artists who display outstanding talent, creativity, and style.

Demand for artists may also depend on the level of government funding for certain programs—for example, the National Endowment for the Arts.

Earnings

As any artist knows, the money doesn't come in regularly, but for those who are persistent, there is money to be made. Sometimes it will come in big chunks. Thus, it is important to learn how to budget your money so it carries you through the times when none seems to be coming in.

Earnings for self-employed visual artists vary widely. Those struggling to gain experience and a reputation may be forced to charge what amounts to less than the minimum wage for their work. Well-established fine artists may earn much more than salaried artists. Self-employed artists do not receive benefits such as paid holidays, sick leave, health insurance, or pensions.

When starting your own studio, you can set things up slowly. A new artist can't usually afford state-of-the art equipment. Secondhand finds are around, and you can build your own workbenches and furniture.

Artists who are lucky to land shows with galleries usually determine with the gallery owner in advance how much each would earn from a sale. Gallery commissions average 50 percent of the sale price. Only the most successful fine artists are able to support themselves solely through sale of their works, however.

Salaries for artisans within living history museums differ depending on whether they are full-time or part-time. The latter group earns an hourly wage ranging between $7.50 and $10.00.

Parade of Professionals

Debra Moss, Freelance Photographer and Writer

"I've always enjoyed photography as a hobby," says Debra Moss, "so I decided to turn it into a career. I worked as a freelance contract archeologist surveyor for five years in Florida, Georgia, and the U.S. Virgin Islands after receiving my master of arts degree in archeology from Ohio State University in Columbus. In 1987, I became a freelance photographer while living in the Virgin Islands. I covered Caribbean travel, yachting, and sailing regattas.

"Then I began searching for a way to add creativity and soul to my life, so I built a portfolio and started sending it out to magazines, hoping to sell my work. Several editors called me and said they loved my photos, but could I write something to go with them? I have always loved writing, so I gave it shot. Soon I was specializing in selling text and photo packages to magazines. I now have more than 150 published credits, including some very well-respected ones, such as *Outside, Bicycling, Yachting,* and many others. I penned columns on computer use for writers, historical and architectural photography, how to shoot sailboat races, and other action sports. I was the press liaison for the internationally known America's Paradise Triathlon on St. Croix.

"My technique is somewhat unique—I use only natural light and have never owned a flash system, so all my work is done outdoors. I try only to capture beauty and have never gone in for what I call the somber side of the profession, photography noir.

"Travel photography, in particular, has allowed me to travel to many places on a magazine's budget. This has probably been the greatest lure. For example, this past March a magazine sent me to Costa Rica to shoot and write an article on surfing. Since I am a surfer, this was quite an enticing offer—and much fun. I love my work, and people are always stunned by the way my camera sees things.

"I took a creative writing class once, but I have no formal education, nor have I ever even taken a photography course. I am told I have an eye, which I believe is an innate ability to see the world in a specific way. (I learned this from a famous photographer who looked at my work and said exactly that—'Well, you certainly have the eye.') After that, it's mostly a matter of learning the mechanics of light, shutter, and lens—the tools of the trade.

"In six years of college, I learned that anything you could ever want to know is in books, so I read every photography book I could find, then went out and shot a hundred rolls of film. That was the sum total of my training.

"Every day is a completely new experience. I don't photograph every day because I work on assignment, but I do write every day. I occasionally go out and shoot for fun so as not to lose sight of the joy I used to feel when I did it only for me and not a paying customer. My husband works at night and I only shoot in the daytime, so sometimes he comes with me and carries my equipment. He is not taken in by the art of what I do particularly, but he enjoys watching me work and going the places it takes me. I am now living near the ocean outside Jacksonville, Florida, and have done numerous articles and photos on Amelia Island for *Ritz Carlton* magazine. Next week I will be taking the ferry to Cumberland Island to interview and photograph the great granddaughter of Thomas Carnegie.

"In a normal week I work about five hours a day, five days a week. The rest of the time I train for triathlons and surf. Not a bad life! The element that bothered me most at first was my insecurity. I hadn't proven to myself that I had earned the right to represent myself as a photographer. My first assignment was scary as I was expected to produce what someone else wanted, and what if I couldn't, or my camera broke, or it rained? It was nerveracking, and I don't like stress much. So over the years I have learned what I can do, what I am pretty good at, and what I can do that hardly anyone else can. That self-knowledge of confidence about my specialties has taken the stress away.

"Secondly, the uncertainty of payment when you freelance almost requires you to have a steady backup income (a spouse or trust fund is nice) or at least a nest egg so that you can go for six months without seeing a dime to get you through until that blissful day when ten checks arrive in the mail together. Other than that, I think being a photographer is just about the neatest profession there is.

"I would recommend that you read everything there is to know, always take your camera with you everywhere you go, and let this wonderful invention take you places you would never have gone."

Carol Revzan, Weaver

"I love to make things," says Carol Revzan, weaver and yarn business owner from Evanston, Illinois. "And it all started when my grandmother taught me to knit and crochet many years ago. After I had been doing so for many years, I saw an antique coverlet, and I knew I had to learn to weave. Several years later, I found a teacher and starting weaving.

"Taking a strand of yarn and manipulating it into fabric or clothing is endlessly fascinating," says Revzan. "The possible combinations of color, texture, and weave structures ensure that I shall never be at a loss for what to do next! Since 1964, I have never been without a project involving yarn or thread. I also love selling yarn and helping people find just that right yarn for their next project.

"I have my studio in my home and work alone. A typical work day starts about 9:00 A.M. and involves weaving until noon with more weaving after lunch. Later in the afternoon, I work on finishing past projects or planning new ones. A good bit of time is

required to design and plan a project before yarn can be thread-
ed onto the loom. I also host once-a-month weaving classes and
always have time for anyone to stop by and purchase yarn.

"What I like most is being able to set my own schedule,
develop designs and projects, and have time to continue to learn
and stretch myself creatively. And do I love taking finished cloth
off the loom!

"What I like least is the fact that this kind of work is a bit
lonely at times and that it's hard to get a good financial return
for the time and effort put into handwoven things.

"I would tell others that good weaving techniques are essential and that a background in color theory and art are most helpful. Though it's difficult to make a living at it, combined with
other activities, it can be very rewarding."

Dave Knoderer, Artist

Dave Knoderer is a self-employed artist based in Sarasota,
Florida. His artistic nickname is "Letterfly." He attended the
University of Southern Illinois at Carbondale and then was an
artist apprentice for several years. He keeps up with his education
by attending several annual workshops and maintaining mem-
berships in several art-related associations. Letterfly's marketing
materials describe him this way: "Letterfly is the top producer of
the high-quality airbrushed murals seen on the outsides of luxury
motorhomes. Wildlife and animal depictions provide the main-
stay for these works. In addition to paintwork on the exterior of
motorhomes, the artist also produces mural work found in homes
and oil paintings on canvas."

"As a child, I was encouraged to create—and painting and
exhibit building are natural for me," says Knoderer. "I was
attracted to the profession by the ability to provide a service
to almost anyone (at the beginning) in about any location. I
enjoyed the freedom to be creative and explore this wonderful

land of ours and provide a service to everyone. The most fulfilling part of my job is experiencing the magnitude of joy that my customers have as the result of my completing a painting for them. Many times it is a genuine honor for me to be painting an intimate part of these special people. My love of my fellow man coupled with sharing my gift with them is very fulfilling.

"I began as a drummer, learned how to travel successfully, and received much satisfaction from being creative and entertaining. But since the creation of art is more concrete, generating a wider audience and a larger demand, my emigration was inevitable. I also enjoy my horses and find the developing of a highly trained dancing horse another artistic form that is strictly spontaneous, in contrast to a painted piece that is timely. One art form complements the other, and I continue with them both to this day.

"How many hours do I work on my art in a week? The early career days were typically spent being creative. As my ability developed, I found that in order to reach another audience (one that would appreciate the level I had achieved), I had to be involved in more and more marketing. Today I spend about a quarter of my time just communicating with people and writing stories and getting publicity in the right places and less and less time (it seems) behind a brush. When I do work, I am focused and I pour all I have into the project. Perhaps the new blend of investing my time is better for the diversification of creation.

"Thanks to my itinerant lifestyle, every job is like an adventure. I never know if I am going to have to trudge through the mud at a current construction site to get to work on the mural I have been commissioned to do or if I have been provided with a spacious shop to begin the project in the midst of luxury.

"The creative energy I have is satisfied when I am asked for my ideas. It seems that of all I do, it is the having of ideas that elevates me above my peers and makes me a person in demand. Oddly enough, the having of ideas isn't what earns any money; it is only after the idea is presented as a plan and executed as a finished work that it realizes any income. Being itinerant is good in that it allows me to be very selective about the jobs I want to do, and that has a lot to do with the success I have enjoyed. The bad side is that I do not have the permanence in the community I desire, and I have no family. I am sure that when I meet my soul mate it will be time to make some more appropriate changes, and then I will choose to travel less.

"Tremendous sacrifice is what it took for me to get to the level of ability that I enjoy today. Dedication and perspiration are also essential ingredients. Becoming an artist and the ability to give of this wonderful gift have always been paramount to me. Perhaps the most despised part of the artistic life is the business end. In the early stages of my career, I was very naive. As a result, I was taken advantage of. Potential and practicing artists should be aware that a strong business head is a tremendous asset."

For More Information

American Arts Alliance
1319 F Street NW, Suite 500
Washington, DC 20004

American Craft Council
Information Center
72 Spring Street
New York, NY 10012

National Museum of American History
Smithsonian Institution, Room 5035
Washington, DC 20560

Costume Society of America
55 Edgewater Drive
P.O. Box 73
Earleville, MD 21919

The National Association of Schools of Art and Design
11250 Roger Bacon Drive, Suite 21
Reston, VA 22090

National Assembly of Local Arts Agencies
927 Fifteenth Street NW, Twelfth Floor
Washington, DC 20005

National Assembly of State Arts Agencies
1010 Vermont Avenue NW, Suite 920
Washington, DC 20005

About the Author

J an Goldberg's love for the printed page began well before her second birthday. Regular visits to the book bindery where her grandfather worked produced a magic combination of sights and smells that she carries with her to this day.

Childhood was filled with composing poems and stories, reading books, and playing library. Elementary and high school included an assortment of contributions to school newspapers. While a full-time college student, Goldberg wrote extensively as part of her job responsibilities in the College of Business Administration at Roosevelt University in Chicago. After receiving a degree in elementary education, she was able to extend her love of reading and writing to her students.

Goldberg has written extensively in the occupations area for General Learning Corporation's *Career World Magazine*, as well as for the many career publications produced by CASS Communications. She has also contributed to a number of projects for educational publishers, including Free Spirit Publishing, Capstone Publishing, Publications International, Scott Foresman, Addison-Wesley, and Camp Fire Boys and Girls.

As a feature writer, Goldberg's work has appeared in *Parenting Magazine, Today's Chicago Woman, Friendly Exchange Magazine, Correspondent Magazine, Chicago Parent, Opportunity Magazine, Successful Student, Complete Woman, North Shore Magazine*, and the Pioneer Press newspapers. Additionally, she has written articles for a number of on-line websites, including Arthur Andersen's Knowledgespace.com and onhealth.com. In all, she has published more than four hundred pieces as a full-time freelance writer.

In addition to *Careers for Geniuses and Other Gifted Types*, she is the author of *Careers for Patriotic Types and Others Who Want to Serve Their Country*, *Careers for Extroverts and Other Gregarious Types*, *Careers in Journalism—2nd Edition*, *Careers for Class Clowns and Other Engaging Types*, *Careers for Color Connoisseurs and Other Visual Types*, *Careers for Competitive Spirits and Other Peak Performers*, *On the Job: Real People Working in Communications*, *On the Job: Real People Working in Entertainment*, *Great Jobs for Music Majors*, *Great Jobs for Theater Majors*, *Great Jobs for Computer Science Majors*, *Careers for Courageous People and Other Adventurous Types*, *Careers in Journalism*, *Great Jobs for Accounting Majors*, *On the Job: Real People Working in Science*, *Opportunities in Research and Development Careers*, *Opportunities in Entertainment Careers*, and *Opportunities in Horticulture Careers*, all published by NTC/Contemporary Publishing Group, Inc.

Goldberg also serves as a writing workshop leader for both children and adults.